The Practical Guide to the
Level 3 Award in Education and Training

Edition 3.0

Contents

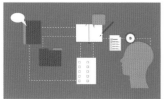

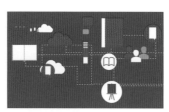

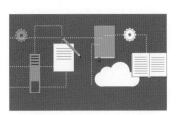

Introduction

In this chapter we will discuss:

- Teaching in education and training
- Professional standards for teachers and trainers in education and training
- Who's who in the Education and Training sector
- The Level 3 Award in Education and Training
- How to use this guide
- Reflective practice

Introduction

Welcome to the Practical Guide to the Level 3 Award in Education and Training. The qualification is designed for anyone teaching or wishing to teach in the Education and Training sector in colleges, industry, business or the public services.

To keep it simple throughout this guide:

- teaching, training, lecturing, tutoring, instructing and coaching are all referred to as **teaching**

- the person carrying out the teaching is referred to as the **teacher**

- those who are learning are referred to as **learners**

Teaching in education and training

What brings you into teaching? Perhaps you have something you are passionate about and want to pass on that knowledge and skill to others; perhaps you feel you can inspire others and delight in seeing them learn, helping to open their minds to something new or gaining a new skill. If you have been teaching for a while, how you teach may be influenced by how you have been taught in the past. Teaching in the Education and Training sector is an immensely rewarding career.

This guide and the course you are undertaking will give you new ideas on how to teach in an inclusive, motivating and professional manner. There are many ways in which we can deliver information (teaching approaches) and we all learn in a variety of ways (learning styles and approaches). Teaching and learning may take place anywhere – on a factory floor, outdoors, in a vehicle, via the internet and not just in a classroom!

> **"Choose a job you love and you will never have to work a day in your life"**
> *Confucius (551BC)*

Professional standards for teachers and trainers in education and training

It is estimated that three quarters of learners are over 19 years old (*Francis and Gould, 2009*). Following concerns that some learners were being taught by unqualified and inexperienced staff, new standards were introduced in September 2007 for all those teaching government funded programmes, including all post-16 education, further education, adult, community-based and work-based learning.

In England, the PTLLS qualification (Preparing to Teach in the Lifelong Learning Sector) became the minimum requirement for all new teachers and the 'threshold qualification', that is the first step in professional qualifications, for those teaching government-funded courses. The Level 3 Award in Education and Training replaces the PTLLS award after a review of qualifications for teachers and trainers by the Learning and Skills Improvement Service (LSIS) in 2012.

Who's who in the Education and Training sector

Office of Qualifications and Examinations Regulation (Ofqual) England.
Council for the Curriculum, Examinations and Assessment (CCEA) Northern Ireland.
The Scottish Qualifications Authority (SQA) Scotland.
Qualifications Wales.

These are the qualification regulatory bodies responsible for overseeing general and vocational qualifications, examinations and assessments in England, Northern Ireland, Scotland and Wales.

Standard Setting Bodies (SSB) or the Sector Skills Council (SSC)

These are the organisations responsible for developing national occupational standards and qualifications.

Regulated Qualifications Framework (RQF)
Qualifications and Credit Framework (QCF) (replaced by RQF Oct 2015)
National Qualifications Framework (NQF) (replaced by RQF Oct 2015)
Scottish Credit and Qualifications Framework (SCQF)
Credit and Qualifications Framework Wales (CQFW)
European Qualifications Framework (EQF)

These are the frameworks recognising and accrediting qualifications in England, Wales, Northern Ireland, Scotland and Europe.

Education and Training Foundation (ETF)

The Education and Training Foundation were set up to improve professionalism in the Further Education (FE) and Skills sectors. In 2013, the Learning and Skills Improvement Service (LSIS) ceased and transferred its legacy to the Education and Training Foundation. In 2014, the Institute for Learning (IfL) also ceased and passed its legacy to the Education and Training Foundation.

Awarding organisations

These are organisations approved by the qualification regulatory bodies to award qualifications. All learners register for a qualification with an awarding organisation and are awarded credits upon successful completion.

External Quality Assurer (EQA)

This is the person approved by the awarding organisation to monitor the work of the approved training centre. The EQA acts as the link between the awarding organisation and the approved centre by working closely with the Internal Quality Assurers (IQAs) and Head of Centre to ensure that the quality of assessment meets the national standard.

Approved Centres – The training organisation approved by the awarding organisation to offer training courses and assessments.

Roles in teaching, learning and assessing

Teacher	Internal Quality Assurer (IQA)
The teacher delivers the course to the learners and collects all required evidence for the course.	The person designated by the approved teaching organisation to ensure the quality and standard of assessing.
Learners	**Assessor**
Those who are enrolled on the course with the approved teaching organisation working towards gaining their units and qualifications.	The assessor is the person who continuously evaluates the aspects of teaching to ensure quality. The assessor may be the teacher delivering the course or someone approved by the training and awarding organisations.

Adapted from Read, H. (2013), *The best assessor's guide (2nd edition)*, Bideford, UK.

The Level 3 Award in Education and Training

The Level 3 Award in Education and Training has 3 mandatory units. Learning at this level involves gaining detailed knowledge and skills and requires the learner to apply these where relevant. The qualification is designed as an introductory teaching qualification to prepare learners for employment. For those learners already in employment, it provides an opportunity for career progression.

During the course you will be expected to research:

* your specialist subject

* the practice of teaching in general

* the practice of teaching your specialist subject

You do not need to be in a teaching role to do certain units of your Level 3 Award in Education and Training but you will need to be involved in at least one hour of microteaching (short teaching sessions). Delivery of your lesson must be a minimum of 15 minutes with the observation and feedback of others making up the remaining 45 minutes. Your course provider will inform you how much contact time you will have with your tutor and how many hours of study you will need to complete in your own time to gain your Level 3 Award in Education and Training. They will also provide information relating to any specific requirements of the awarding organisation.

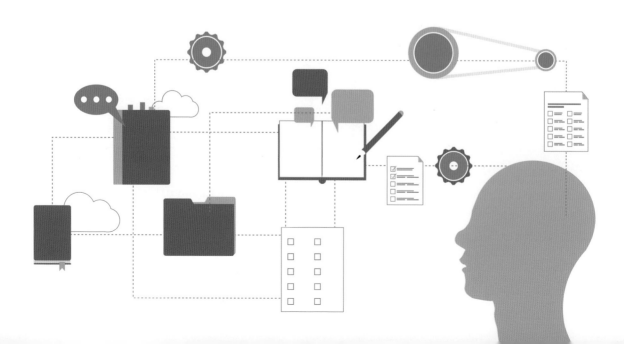

How to use this guide

This guide provides ideas and information to help you throughout the course:

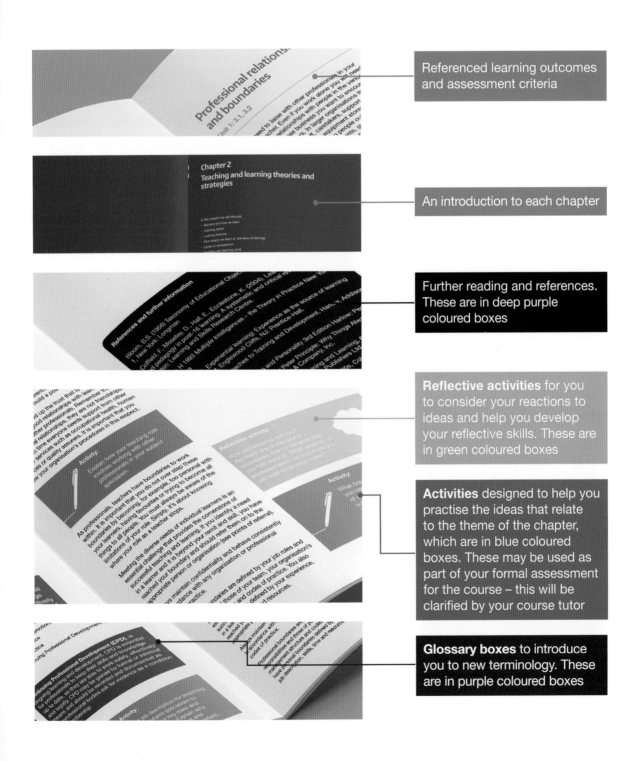

Referenced learning outcomes and assessment criteria

An introduction to each chapter

Further reading and references. These are in deep purple coloured boxes

Reflective activities for you to consider your reactions to ideas and help you develop your reflective skills. These are in green coloured boxes

Activities designed to help you practise the ideas that relate to the theme of the chapter, which are in blue coloured boxes. These may be used as part of your formal assessment for the course – this will be clarified by your course tutor

Glossary boxes to introduce you to new terminology. These are in purple coloured boxes

This guide is written to cover all the essentials you will need. It is written in plain English, to guide you through the units required to gain your Level 3 Award in Education and Training. It covers all the learning outcomes and assessment criteria of the Level 3 Award in Education and Training and is laid out in chapters that correspond to the main sections of study for the theory aspects of the award:

1. Understanding roles, responsibilities and relationships in education and training.

2. Understanding and using inclusive teaching and learning approaches in education and training.

3. Understanding assessment in education and training.

The units are detailed in the Appendix at the back of this guide. Each unit has been given a number: 1 – 3.

Please note this numbering is solely for the purpose of this guide to clarify the assessment criteria each section is fulfilling. When referring to these units in other books, qualification specifications or websites, please refer to the unit title and unit reference number of each.

There are three units from the Learning and Development NVQ qualifications that are accepted for the new Level 3 Award in Education and Training:

o Facilitate learning and development for individuals (6 credits)

o Facilitate learning and development in groups (6 credits)

o Understanding the principles and practices of assessment (3 credits)

If you have achieved one or more of these already, check with your course tutor as to how these qualifications may be used as evidence for credit transfer or Recognition of Prior Learning (RPL) towards your teaching qualification.

Each unit has learning outcomes and assessment criteria:

Learning outcomes – state what the learner will know, understand and do as a result of their learning.

Assessment criteria – state how the learner will demonstrate that the learning criteria have been met. Where the assessment criteria are covered, they are referenced like so – Unit 1: 1.1

This guide is written with new teachers in mind, as a source of information on the practice of teaching. It is your responsibility to ensure you are up to date with your specialist subject.

Reflective practice

Reflective practice is simply you thinking about what you will do, are doing and have done in your teaching practice and activities in your subject specialism. Reflective practice is an important part of a professional's life.

The key purposes of reflective practice are:

- to identify new learning needs or opportunities for learning

- to solve problems, or find another way of doing something

- for personal and professional development

- to demonstrate competencies

- to escape routine practice (simply 'because it's always been done this way' for example)

- to identify areas of practice and routine that work very well ('don't make changes for changes sake')

One of the best ways to record your reflections is in diary form commonly known as a Reflective Practice Journal (RPJ). Your RPJ enables you to reflect on your own practice and experiences in a structured way. Use it to:

- record useful information

- write down your thoughts and ideas

- identify areas you need to work on

- acknowledge your strengths

- record the strengths and weaknesses of others, so that you can use it to build on your knowledge and skills

You can also record your personal thoughts, feelings and reactions about issues, difficulties and achievements that occur in teaching and activities at work that impact on your teaching.

You can complete your RPJ in various ways, for example in a computer document, diary or an audio log. Make sure you use your RPJ and have two copies, one for your tutor and one for yourself.

References and further information

Francis, M. & Gould, J (2014) *Achieving Your Award in Education and Training*. Sage publications Ltd.

Read, H 2016. *The best assessor's guide*. Bideford: Read On Publications Ltd.

Websites

Education and Training Foundation

Chapter 1
Roles, responsibilities and relationships in education and training

In this chapter we will discuss:

- What makes an effective teacher?
- Roles and responsibilities of a teacher
- Professional relationships and boundaries
- Points of referral
- Legislation, regulation and codes of practice
- Record keeping

Chapter 1
Roles, responsibilities and relationships in education and training

What makes an effective teacher?

"The art of teaching is the art of assisting discovery"

Mark Van Doren – Professor of English at Columbia University 1920-72

Activity:

Take a few moments to list the qualities, both personal and professional, that you think an effective teacher should have. Think about the qualities of those people who have inspired you over the years.

Reflective activity:

Do you have the above qualities?
Can you and do you want to develop them?
Is a career in teaching right for you?

As a teacher, there will be certain personal and professional qualities you possess which will develop more as you practise your teaching skills. You may have some of these qualities in abundance already, others you may need to learn and strengthen as you practise. Teaching is a dedicated profession, sometimes challenging and demanding – it is not something to do half-heartedly. However, passing on your knowledge and skills to others, enabling them to understand and do something new is deeply satisfying. Those who have inspired and helped us in the past are never forgotten.

There are two categories of teaching role in the sector and you should aspire to gain one of these statuses:

- **Associate Teacher, Learning and Skills (ATLS)** – this role has fewer teaching responsibilities and will usually use materials prepared by someone else.

- **Qualified Teacher, Learning and Skills (QTLS)** – this role has all the responsibilities of a full teaching role, performing all the aspects of the teaching and learning cycle.

Roles and responsibilities of a teacher

Unit 1: 1.1

As a teacher you must be aware of:

- your *roles* – your job, function and position within your organisation as a teacher

- your *responsibilities* – the things that you have the authority to carry out and that you are accountable or answerable for

- your *boundaries* – the limitations of your role, your organisation and professional code of practice

Your main role as a teacher is to deliver your subject lessons in an effective way that stimulates, includes and involves all of your learners. You need to communicate with your learners on their level, in terms they will understand and then gradually develop and increase their knowledge and skills as they progress.

You will also need to assess how well they are learning throughout each lesson and manage their learning from the beginning to the end of their course.

An effective teacher will do these things with enthusiasm and passion for their subject and be approachable to all learners, valuing diversity and creating a positive relationship with their learners and other professionals in their organisation. They ensure their professional skills are kept up to date and continue to aim for improvement through reflective practice. They manage their time well and are aware of their professional and personal boundaries.

Your learners will place a great deal of trust in you and that trust is central to the relationship between you the teacher and your learners.

You will be working with other professionals directly or indirectly. Professional standards and conduct need to be maintained here too. All the professionals in a team must have a clear knowledge of their own roles and responsibilities to help create positive working relationships and an effective team. If you are ever in any doubt as to whether or not something is your responsibility, you should check with someone in your organisation, for example your line manager. If you have your own training company and work on your own, you can check with a professional organisation or another similar company.

Depending on where and what you are teaching, you will have many roles and responsibilities. For example:

Roles – what I am

- Teacher
- Organiser and planner
- Ambassador for my organisation
- Mediator and facilitator
- Administrator
- Assessor
- Manager or team leader
- Coach
- Trainer
- Mentor
- Instructor
- Lecturer

Responsibilities – what I do

- Carry out learner inductions and initial assessments
  - Teach well-informed, inclusive and motivating lessons using a variety of appropriate teaching, learning and assessment methods and resources.
  - Meet individual learner needs to give all learners an equal opportunity to learn
  - Give constructive feedback
- Tutorials
  - Carry out assessments as required by my organisation and the awarding organisation
- Maintain duty of care
  - Refer learners to specialist agencies or other professionals when appropriate
  - Abide by relevant legislation, regulations and guidelines
- Evaluate lessons or courses
  - Record keeping in accordance with the requirements of my organisation, the awarding organisation and the Data Protection Act 2018. General Data Protection Regulation (GDPR)
  - Communicate effectively
- Attend meetings and professional interactions and discussions
- Attend area and national conferences, promotional events and exhibitions
  - Abide by professional codes of practice
- Undertake and record reflective practice
- Plan, carry out and record Continuing Professional Development (CPD)

Continuing Professional Development (CPD), is ongoing learning and development. CPD is essential for professionals to keep their skills and knowledge up to date, so they are able to work safely, effectively and legally. CPD may be gained by formal or informal means and should be recorded and documented as all professional bodies ask for evidence as a condition of membership.

Activity:

Use a job description for teaching in your subject specialism to highlight your key roles and responsibilities. Explain why you think these roles and responsibilities are important.

Professional relationships and boundaries

Unit 1: 3.1, 3.2

You will need to liaise with other professionals in your role as a teacher. Even if you work alone you will need to build good relationships with people in the venues you use and whose business you want to encourage, not just your learners. In larger organisations there are administration staff, caretakers, support workers, technicians, staff in your equipment stores, other teachers, etc. There are also people outside the organisation, for example parents, guardians, employers, with whom you'll want to build a positive relationship.

You should aim to build up the trust that is essential if you are to have good relationships with learners, colleagues and other professionals. Remember these are professional relationships, they are not friendships. From time to time everyone needs support from other people or services such as occupational health, human resources or quality assurers. It is important that you follow your organisation's procedures in this respect.

To be successful and effective, an organisation needs all its' professionals to work within these boundaries, helping to create positive working relationships and effective lines of communication. Staying within your boundaries makes your duty to perform your roles easier and treat all fairly without favouritism or prejudice.

Activity:

Explain how your teaching role involves working with other professionals in your subject specialism.

As professionals, teachers have boundaries to work within. It is important that you do not overstep these boundaries by becoming, for example, too personal with your learners, having favourites or trying to become all things to all people. You must always be aware of the limitations of your role. Simply, it's about knowing where your role as a teacher stops.

Meeting the diverse needs of individual learners is an essential challenge that provides the cornerstone of successful teaching and learning. If you identify a need in a learner and it is beyond your remit and skill, you have reached your boundary and should refer them on to the appropriate person or organisation (see Points of referral, page 20).

Always maintain confidentiality and behave consistently in accordance with any organisation or professional codes of practice.

Professional boundaries are defined by your job roles and responsibilities and those of your team, your organisation's management structure and codes of practice. You also have personal boundaries defined by your experience, job description, skills, time and resources.

Reflective activity:

How professional are you? Are there any professional boundaries and constraints that you find testing? What aspects of professionalism do you think you will need to develop more?

Activity:

What boundaries do you think you need to be particularly aware of when teaching your specialist subject? Give examples of where boundaries may be crossed. How can you ensure that you stay within your professional boundaries?

Points of referral

Unit 1: 3.3

You cannot be all things to all people, nor can you be the fount of all knowledge. Knowing who to ask and when is a sensible, responsible and professional attitude to adopt. Always aim to act before something becomes a bigger problem. Sometimes you will need to refer a learner on to another professional or organisation. The specialist may be someone within your organisation, for example specialist tutor, Occupational Health Department, or, in the public realm, for example General Practitioner, counselling service, Citizen's Advice Bureau or local council.

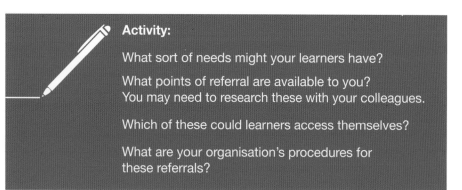

Activity:

What sort of needs might your learners have?

What points of referral are available to you?
You may need to research these with your colleagues.

Which of these could learners access themselves?

What are your organisation's procedures for these referrals?

Legislation, regulations and codes of practice

Unit 1: 1.2

All professionals need to keep up to date with current legislation, regulations and codes of practice (sometimes called codes of ethics or conduct).

Legislation – laws passed by legislative bodies, for example government, city council.

Regulations – rules that govern procedure/behaviour and dictate how legislation should be carried out.

Codes of practice – authorised guidance that explains how people working in a particular profession should behave set by their professional organisation.

Some examples of legislation are:

The Equality Act 2010 became law in October 2010. It replaces previous legislation (such as the Race Relations Act 1976 and the Disability Discrimination Act 1995) and ensures consistency in what you need to do to make your workplace a fair environment for all.

The Equality Act 2010 covers the same groups that were protected by the previous equality legislation – age, disability, gender reassignment, race, religion or belief, sex, sexual orientation, marriage and civil partnership and pregnancy and maternity – but extends some protections to groups not previously covered, and also strengthens particular aspects of equality law.

The Health and Safety at Work Act 1974 (HASAWA) ensures that organisations have policies and procedures in place that requires them by law to protect staff, learners, customers and visitors from illness or injury as much as is reasonably practical. Each establishment must do its own risk assessments. Only when the necessary preventative measures and the right equipment and training have been employed is it a safe environment where people are genuinely safe to work and learn.

All staff need to be aware of the health and safety regulations and recommendations in their workplace. As a teacher it is your responsibility to ensure that you and your learners are in a suitable venue, any equipment being used is in good working order and in the event of a fire everyone knows where the fire exits and meeting points are. Learners also need to know where toilets are, where they can get food and refreshments and if there are any health and safety considerations relevant to their specific industry/environment (if relevant to the course or venue). These may seem like minor issues but they have a big impact on learning and represent utmost concern in providing a safe context for our work, its effectiveness, and one that also protects from charges of negligence.

Health and safety policy statement

Health and Safety at Work etc. Act 1974

This is the Health and Safety Policy Sta

_____

(name of company)

Our statement of general policy

- to provide adequate contr
  activities;
- to consult with c
- to provide and
- to ensure safe ha
- to provide informatic

Data Protection Act 2018. General Data Protection Regulation (GDPR)
The Data Protection Act updates our data protection laws for the digital age. It preserves existing tailored exemptions that have worked well in the former Data Protection Act 1998 which was developed to give protection and lay down rules about how much data about people can be used, how it is stored and how long it may be kept for.

The Protection of Children Act 1999 (POCA) gives responsibility to local authorities to make enquiries when anyone contacts them with concerns about child abuse.

Safeguarding Vulnerable Adults Act 2006 – If you are teaching children or vulnerable adults, or at premises where there are children or vulnerable adults present, you may need to obtain a Disclosure and Barring Service (DBS) certificate before working on the premises (previously known as a CRB certificate – formally the Criminal Records Bureau).

Activity:

Research and summarise the main legislations, regulations and codes of practice relevant to your roles and responsibilities in particular the E&T foundation's Professionals Standards 2014.

Examples of other regulations include:

Control of Substances Hazardous to Health (COSHH) Provides regulations for those who work with hazardous materials.

Reporting of Injuries, Diseases & Dangerous Occurrences Regulations 2013 (RIDDOR) requires employers (including the self employed) or those in control of premises to report any work-related deaths, specified injuries, occupational diseases, reportable dangerous occurrences and non-fatal accidents requiring hospital treatment to non-workers to the HSE. Injuries that occur at work that mean the worker is absent or unable to do their work for more than 7 days need to be reported within 15 days of the accident occurring. Employers must also keep a record of all injuries that result in workers being unable to work for more than 3 days (an accident book entry is acceptable).

Examples of codes of practice include:

Information Technology Codes of Practice relate to the use of computer technology in your place of work including schools giving guidance for email protocol, intranet and internet access including the boundaries with regard to social media.

The Education and Training Foundation's Professional Standards 2014 cover three areas of equal importance for teachers:

1. Professional values and attributes
2. Professional knowledge and understanding
3. Professional skills

The 2014 professional standards:

- set out clear expectations of effective practice in education and training
- enable teachers and trainers to identify areas for their own professional development
- support initial teacher education
- provide a national reference point that organisations can use to support the development of their staff

National Vocational Qualifications Code of Practice (2006) (*amended 2011*) sets out the responsibilities for awarding organisations and their approved centres for the administration, assessment and quality assurance of National Vocational Qualifications (NVQs) and competence-based units. It was developed to promote quality, consistency, accuracy and fairness in the assessment and awarding of these types of qualifications.

Awarding Organisations Codes of Practice set the guidelines and requirements of teaching and assessment and the behaviour expected of teaching professionals including the use of ICT, social media, timekeeping, dress and organisational specifics.

Record keeping

Unit 1: 1.1 Unit 3: 4.1

Records provide crucial evidence of what was planned, what was done, where and with whom, what was achieved, and what will be done next time. There are records for all aspects of teaching, that is planning, delivery and assessing but also important records for the organisation itself, for example health and safety, grievances, complaints and dispute procedures, equal opportunities and diversity data. Records need to be completed at the right time, for instance, the register of attendance is done at the beginning of the lesson and becomes vitally and immediately important if there's a fire and the building is evacuated. They must be up to date, legible, accurate and factual, kept securely in accordance with The Data Protection Act, electronically, manually or both. Only adequate and relevant information should be kept and for no longer than is necessary. Your organisation will provide guidance on keeping records for them. Record forms should be designed to make life easier. The types of records needed for each stage of planning and teaching are referred to in the appropriate chapter.

References and further information

Websites

Advisory, Conciliation and Arbitration Service

Health and Safety Executive

Education and Training Foundation

Chapter 2
Teaching and learning theories and strategies

In this chapter we will discuss:

- Memory and how we learn
- Learning styles
- Learning theories
- How deeply we learn or 'domains of learning'
- Levels of competence
- Teaching and learning cycle
- Approaches to teaching and learning
- Teaching and learning environments/situations
- Teaching techniques

Chapter 2
Teaching and learning theories and strategies

Unit 2: 2.2

"Experience without theory is blind, but theory without experience is mere intellectual play"

Immanuel Kant – German philosopher 1724-1804

What do you think of theory? How do you feel about it? To some it can seem 'stuffy' and pointless. Why not just get on with the job? There is so much we can offer and precious little time to do it. Why spend so much time and effort researching how people learn or think, when all we need to do is tell people what they need to know?

People are all different and all learn in different ways. To be effective teachers, we need to understand how diverse people are, so that we can truly communicate with each person as an individual. Most of the time, we do communicate in groups, rather than with individuals, so good teachers need to understand how to relate to different learning styles and abilities and also be able to do this with different types of people at the same time.

This means that we need to understand how people learn and how to plan our teaching to meet their learning needs. Without theory, we would not know which aspects of our teaching have worked and why. We would meet some needs but not many and not understand why. We too are learning from our teaching and our learners!

Quite simply, theory helps us to do our job better and to have a greater sense of achievement for those we teach.

The memory and how we learn

Unit 2: 2.2

Understanding a little about how the memory works and the way people learn will help you pass on your knowledge and skills in a suitable way. Everyone learns differently, influenced by experiences throughout their lives. It also helps to know what learners expect to gain or achieve from your teaching. Being aware of any special requirements that learners have, which may stand in the way of learning, will allow you to provide any special support they may need.

As we learn, we use knowledge that we already have and build on it, making new connections and 'grouping' the information into 'chunks', gradually building on these chunks. We often remember blocks as patterns, which is the crux of Gestalt theory. Gestalt literally means pattern or structure. We often think of numbers as patterns too. Think of how you remember your PIN numbers or house alarm number, it'll probably be as a pattern – visual, auditory, written or movement (kinaesthetic). Rather than seeing each block as a separate entity, Gestalt theory looks at the whole picture and the synergy of the overall perspective.

Synergy – The interaction of two or more elements, which when combined produce a result that is greater than the individual elements e.g. a singer accompanied by guitarist or a band.

For example: If you were learning about car engines for the first time and the teacher just said 'find and remove the distributor', you wouldn't know what the distributor looked like, let alone where it was! But, if the teacher showed you a distributor and explained what it does, each of its components, where it is normally situated and how to remove it, then you would be able to locate it, remove it and understand its job. From that point onwards, the teacher only needs to refer to 'a distributor' and you will be able to visualise it, know exactly what it is, what it is for and how to find, remove and replace one. You have sub-consciously grouped the information and individual components together "as a whole". Now you understand it as one thing and it means much more to you than simply thinking of each separate part, that is synergy. Gestalt theory believes that understanding is based on insight and understanding i.e. the 'penny dropping', or a 'eureka' moment or a flash of inspiration.

Memory can be divided into three storage systems (*Anderson 1999*):

- **Sensory Memory** – holds an exact copy of what is seen or heard (visual and auditory) and lasts for a mere few seconds.

- **Short-Term Memory (STM)** – receives information to which we pay particular attention to and so moves from the sensory memory to the STM. STM is mostly stored as sounds, especially in recalling words, but may be stored as images. Only a limited amount of information is transferred from the sensory memory into the STM. It is then transferred to other parts of the memory system or discarded. It is thought that we remember about seven 'chunks' of information. The STM is vulnerable to interruption or interference.

- **Long-Term Memory (LTM)** – is where storage is relatively permanent. Donald Hebb (1968) argued that a chemical process could not occur fast enough to accommodate immediate memory and remain stable enough to accommodate permanent memory.

So, information is stored on the basis of the impact it has made with repetition, meaning, relevance and importance.

Learning styles

Unit 2: 1.2

Everyone learns differently, influenced by experiences throughout their lives. It also helps to know what learners expect to gain or achieve from your teaching. Being aware of any special requirements that learners have will allow you to provide any special support they may need.

Learning styles have been much studied in recent years and aim to help us understand how people learn and understand information. Understanding the ways that people learn will help you to devise and plan good teaching and to deliver it well.

Fleming's learning styles

Neil Fleming's 'VARK' model has been one of the most popular since its creation in 1987 and was updated in 2005. Fleming developed a questionnaire and itemised a list designed to help learners and others, learn more about their individual learning preferences.

Visual learners usually learn best by looking. They would rather watch than do and memorise by using pictures or mental 'video'. Graphic displays such as charts, diagrams, illustrations, handouts and videos are all helpful learning tools for visual learners. They tend to be careful about their appearance and notice the finer details.

Auditory learners usually learn best from listening and enjoy talking. They tend to be responsive to music and often sing, hum and use rhythm to memorise. They get a great deal out of lectures and are good at remembering things they are told. They can be easily distracted and don't like noisy environments.

Reading learners usually learn best from the written word. They tend to make many notes while listening and reading, but prefer to read straight from the textbook. They enjoy making lists. Helpful tools for these learners are definitions, course handouts, PowerPoint and any other text based resources.

Kinaesthetic learners usually learn best from doing and touching. They like physical activity, can be very tactile and will often use their hands when talking. They tend not to be keen on reading or sitting still.

Most learners are a mix of these, or 'multi-modal'. Multi-modal learners tend to learn more quickly than those who are more single-modal.

Honey and Mumford's learning styles

The Activist enjoys the here and now and is usually very enthusiastic. They like quick challenges and learn best from activities where they can throw themselves into new or exciting experiences, or be 'thrown in at the deep end'. They are often quick to volunteer to be in the limelight, to lead discussions, perform or resolve a crisis. They enjoy teamwork but love to be given the opportunity to come up with their own ideas and solutions.

The Reflector likes to explore and think deeply about things before making a conclusion. They like things that have been tried and tested and learn best from activities where they are encouraged to observe, listen, reflect and consider activities. For example, investigate, assemble information and have enough time to think before saying anything. They appreciate the opportunity for feedback or to produce a report.

The Theorist likes principles, theories and systems. They enjoy reading and thinking about something before doing it and they learn best from activities where there are clear rules about how things are done. They like working with ready made ideas and concepts even if they are not relevant straight away, especially if they can test and question to help them think more widely about an issue.

The Pragmatist looks for new ideas and wants to experiment getting their hands dirty as soon as possible. They like logical, useful reasons for doing something and they learn best from activities where the learning is immediately useful for the job in hand, for example, timesaving or how to deal with difficult people. They relish the chance to try out and practice new techniques, particularly with expert guidance from someone they see as a good role model for themselves.

We use all these different learning styles ourselves to a lesser or greater degree. This means that we can use them to support our own learning and that of others. The theory here allows us to better understand our teaching and focus on how we plan and deliver our teaching.

The four styles as stages of learning – Honey and Mumford's Learning Cycle (1986)

Originally Honey and Mumford's Learning Cycle was designed to help people make decisions, complete tasks or resolve problems in business management. Each style is also a stage of learning and the stages relate to the four styles of learning described above.

We may not be aware of some of these in our own thinking and learning. We have to practise using them all so that we can apply ourselves better to teaching, learning and planning.

The Honey and Mumford Learning Styles questionnaire is a tool to discover your mix of styles and can be very helpful in decision making, learning, revising and planning. It shows how important a good understanding of theory can be if we want to be an effective teacher.

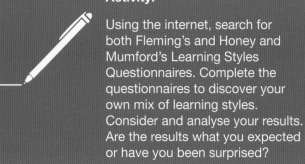

Activity:

Using the internet, search for both Fleming's and Honey and Mumford's Learning Styles Questionnaires. Complete the questionnaires to discover your own mix of learning styles. Consider and analyse your results. Are the results what you expected or have you been surprised?

Why use learning style theories and questionnaires?

- Do learners learn best when teaching methods match their strongest learning style?

- Will they do better in education when activities are aligned to their learning strengths and preferences?

Studying teaching and learning theory may, to those theorists among you, seem incredibly interesting, or to those activists amongst you, seem tedious. However, if we know how we and our learners learn best, our efforts as teachers can be more effective. Learning to apply theory to practice can be an interesting and rewarding process.

Frank Coffield (2005) argues that assessing the individual learning styles of all learners is without any real value as existing research has found that simply matching teaching methods to learning styles has no influence on educational outcomes. The argument here is that it is enough for a teacher to know that different learners will have different preferred learning styles. But here lies the real usefulness of learning styles questionnaires, as most people are a mixture of learning styles, not just one. If you know how your learners learn best, you can help them to learn better by adjusting your teaching to their own way of learning.

So, it is of utmost importance to use a variety of teaching methods to accommodate all learning styles, all of the time, wherever possible.

A teacher needs to be aware of their own preferred learning styles too, a trap that must be avoided is to presume that all learners learn something in the same way as you do. By using a variety of teaching methods to accommodate all learning styles, learners will have the opportunity to learn effectively via their own preferred style, as well as having weaker learning styles exercised and strengthened. This is essential for their development.

In understanding their own learning style preferences, learners can facilitate their own learning and revision. For example, if a learner knows that visual learning appeals to them most, they can use visual study aids to help them remember the information they are studying. However, what we learn from the learning cycles and knowing is that we have a mix of learning styles, is that learning a subject is easiest and most effective when we use a range of different approaches, for example, explanation, demonstration, practice, being coached, revision or reflection.

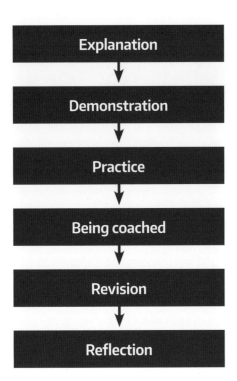

This reinforces the learning and helps the learner retain the information for longer. Knowing your learners' styles will help you plan your lessons and assessments more effectively. If you have time on courses, it is very useful to get your learners to fill in a learning style questionnaire. It's fun, informative and motivating; people love learning about themselves!

Reflective activity:

What have you learnt about yourself from your learning style questionnaire results? How can you use this new knowledge to aid your own learning? How can you develop those styles that are currently weaker? Reflect on how your preferred learning styles may affect your teaching in a positive or a challenging way.

Learning theories

Unit 2: 2.1

Experiential theory – Kolb's Learning Cycle (1984):

Kolb's Experiential Learning theory on how adults learn and develop is one of the most significant. He suggests that people learn from their experiences. They have the experience, then think about it, then they are able to adapt or change their behaviour as a result. He proposed a four stage cycle of learning.

Concrete experience is the 'doing' stage; actually experiencing and feeling the event or task assigned.

Observation and reflection is the 'thinking about it' stage. Beliefs, values and attitudes will influence how you review the event.

Abstract conceptualization is the 'planning of how you will do it next time' stage. Assimilation, critically analysing and interpreting the experience will make sense of the event or task so that next time you can apply the wisdoms learned the last time.

Active experimentation is the 're-doing' stage. Predicting and planning how the task/event will run next time with the value of experience and reflection.

Kolb's Experiential Learning Cycle provides the basic approach of most adult and further education lessons. Allowing learners to undertake tasks can reinforce their learning through experience and reflection. Without reflection we can continue to miss what's good, become out of date, or make the same mistakes. You also need to reflect on your own teaching and learning. Without reflection you cannot know if your teaching is productive, pertinent or enjoyable.

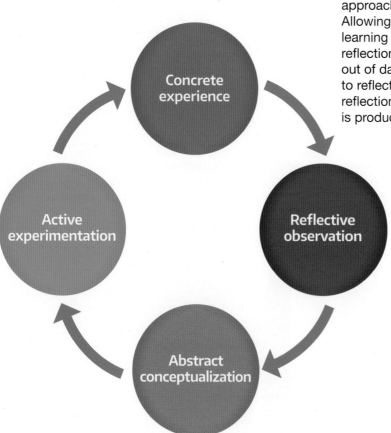

Comparing Kolb's and Honey and Mumford's Learning Cycles

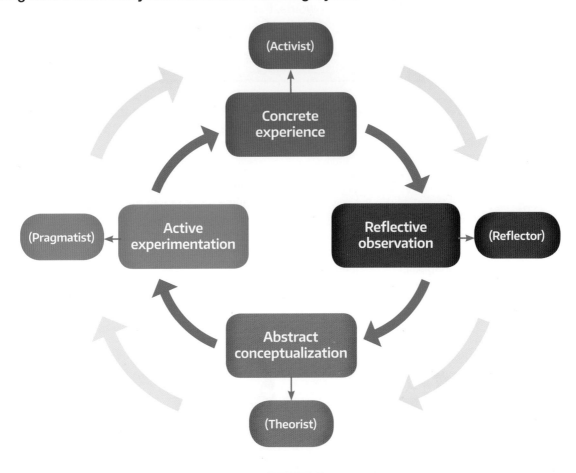

Reflective activity:

Compare Kolb's learning cycle to that of Honey and Mumford. What similarities do you notice? Are you aware of any key differences in these approaches? How can these learning cycles help you reflect on the effectiveness of your teaching?

Other learning theories that may interest you are:

- **Zone of Proximal Development (ZPD) – Vygotsky (1978)**

- **Behaviourist Theory – Skinner (1974)**

- **Humanist Theory – Rogers (1983)**

- **Sensory Theory – Laird (1985)**

- **Intelligences – Howard Gardner (1992)**

How deeply we learn or 'domains of learning'

Unit 2: 2.2, 2.3, 3.2, 4.1

> **"All our talents increase in the using; and every faculty, both good and bad, strengthens by exercise"**
>
> *Anne Bronte (1820-49)*

Domains of learning can be simply described as theories that look at how deeply we learn something, in other words, that what is learnt is fully understood and can be applied. Our learning goes through stages, or depths of learning.

Domain – an area or scope of knowledge or activity

We learn best when we are interested in the subject, perhaps because it is relevant, meaningful, and/or there is an immediate benefit to learning. It is worth looking at how we learn new things.

Benjamin Bloom (1956) disagreed that education was about merely learning facts; he believed that it is about mastery (deep learning) of knowledge, skills and attitudes. To learn something new, he claims that we need to pay attention, which may seem like stating the obvious. But it's in paying attention that we can 'receive' and understand what is being taught. This helps our memory to select the important information to remember long term. He recognised too, that when we learn we are affected and engaged in three different ways or 'domains', simply thinking, feeling and doing. He called these domains:

Cognitive
(thinking or head)

Affective
(emotions or heart)

Psychomotor
(actions or hands)

When the three domains are engaged in learning, using a holistic approach, the learning is deeper and longer term. Each domain has levels of learning and understanding and is known as Bloom's 'Taxonomy', or classification. The taxonomy classifies learning and thinking into six levels of complexity, which are knowledge, comprehension, application, analysis, synthesis, and evaluation.

Bloom's Taxonomy

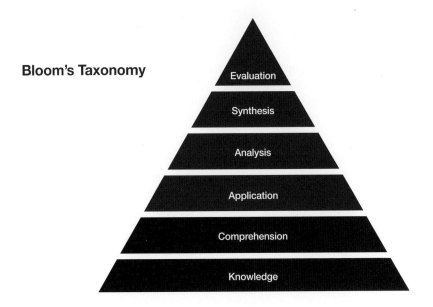

Anderson and Krathwohl's Revision of the Taxonomy

The levels are often depicted as a stairway or pyramid, inspiring many teachers to encourage their learners to aim for a higher level of thought and understanding. When learners have mastered a skill or gained some knowledge, only then has the teacher done a good job! Simply, we know a learner has truly mastered something when they:

- can recognise

- can show they understand

- are able to apply the skill or knowledge to a real-life situation

- are able to use the new information to analyse a real life situation

In 2001, Anderson and Krathwohl researched and revised the domains of learning and suggested new descriptions for the six levels. These new levels are; remembering, understanding, applying, analysing, evaluating, and creating.

Activity:

Choose an area of your specialist subject and consider how you might teach it. Which domain is most affected by the subject area? Can you think of ways to engage the other domains of learning into this area? Why is it important to engage all three domains of learning?

Reflective activity:

Think of the skills that your learners need to gain in your specialist area. These skills may be practical, for example bricklaying; oral or aural, for example speaking another language; or cognitive, for example calculations. How have you been taught those skills? Do you think it would have been easier to learn if they were taught in a different way?

How might you go about teaching those skills?

The four stages of competence

As Bloom suggests, true learning has been achieved when the learner is competent at the skill or subject.

> **Competence** – being capable; the ability to perform a skill

Peter and Hull (1969) suggest that learners can only achieve a higher level of learning when they are competent at the level before.

The levels of competency are;

Unconscious incompetence: This stage is when a learner doesn't know that they don't know. Perhaps they are unaware of a skill or knowledge needed for a new role. (Sometimes there are those who think they are competent at a skill but are not. We can all think of a 'Smart Alec' who thinks they are the most competent person around or someone whose skills have diminished over time and does not realise. Usually people become aware of their own incompetence becoming a 'conscious incompetent' and open to learning). To progress, the learner *needs to know what it is that they don't know*.

Conscious incompetence: This is a mostly transitional stage; a learner is aware of the gap in their knowledge or skills and knows what they need to learn to become competent. Often learners start at this stage.

Conscious competence: The learner is competent and knows it. At this stage the conscious competent may need to really concentrate while performing the new skill or need frequent reassurance. More practice will move them on to the next level.

Unconscious competence: The learner is unaware of how competent they are. They are so used to doing it they don't have to think about it, the skills have become easy and 'second nature'. At this stage they will need stretching further, or they may get bored.

The aim of teaching is to assist the learner to become an unconscious competent in any skills being passed on, and then show them the next stage of learning or a new skill, where they realise they are incompetent (conscious incompetent) again and that there is more to learn.

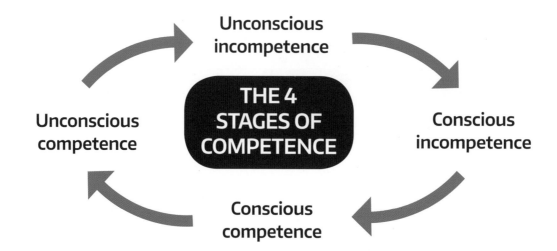

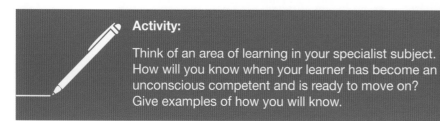

Activity:

Think of an area of learning in your specialist subject. How will you know when your learner has become an unconscious competent and is ready to move on? Give examples of how you will know.

> "The greatest sign of success for a teacher is to be able to say, 'The children are now working as if I did not exist'."
>
> *Maria Montessori – Italian Physician and Educator 1870-1952*

Teaching and learning cycle

Unit 1: 1.1

The teaching and learning cycle consists of five stages:

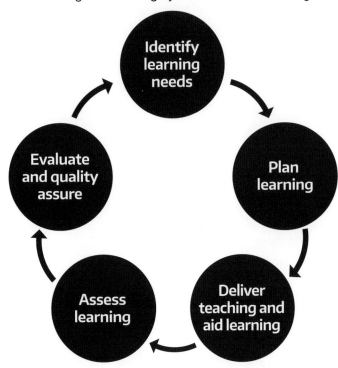

Knowing the principles of the teaching and learning cycle will help you plan ahead. Teaching and learning must follow through all these stages for both to be effective. Both the teacher and the learner have responsibility to ensure each stage has been achieved. Once the cycle has been completed it can continue with further study and increased awareness of the needs of the learner.

Identify learner needs – what are the needs of your learners, yourself and your organisation? Applications and enrolment processes and initial assessments of learners will give you this information and enable you to agree their Individual Learning Plans (ILPs).

IPL – a specific learning plan for an individual's program of learning, taking into account their learning needs and talents.

Plan learning – ensures your schemes of work and lesson plans are ready for your course or lessons. Prepare and have ready the teaching, learning and assessment resources that you will use. This may involve working with others.

Deliver teaching and aid learning – use the best teaching and learning approaches for your learners with well chosen resources. Aim to make your learners' learning straightforward and set at the correct level, so that they can learn as much as possible from each of your lessons.

Assess learning – check that your learners have gained the knowledge and skills intended, for example, you may lead and invigilate a formal assessment.

Evaluate and quality assure – Obtain evaluations from your learners, possibly others and yourself so that you can judge the success of your methods, resources and organisation. From these, decide if alterations and improvements can be made to the lesson or the course. Evaluation is an ongoing process and can occur at any point.

Record keeping and the teaching and learning cycle

There are records at every stage of the teaching and learning cycle. Examples include:

- Identify learner needs: application forms, induction forms, learning style results, induction forms

ULN – a personal 10-digit number allocated to a learner by the Learning Records Service (LRS). The ULN remains with the learner throughout their life meaning all future credits and qualifications are linked together.

- Plan learning: schemes of work, lesson plans, ILPs

- Deliver teaching and aid learning: attendance registers, accident report forms, tutorial reviews.

- Assess learning: assessment plans, assessment forms and marking sheets, learner evaluation forms, evidence of course work and portfolios.

- Evaluate and quality assure: Internal Quality Assurer (IQA) and External Quality Assurer (EQA) reports, minutes of meetings, CPD records, registration and certification data, equal opportunities data, teacher's lesson evaluations.

These records support the learning process and provide essential information for internal and external quality assurers, regulators, inspectors etc.

Approaches to teaching and learning

Unit 2: 1.2

Pedagogical and Andragogical approaches

Ped-a-gog-i-cal approach – 'teacher-led'

Teachers assume responsibility for the teaching process, making all the decisions on content, style and teaching methods used.

In the pedagogical approach, the teacher decides what is being taught and how. The learners have little input in to how lessons are taught.

As adults mature they become more accustomed to making their own decisions and directing their own path in life. They may therefore put up a resistance and resent being 'told' what to do in a learning situation. They may prefer a learning environment in which they are allowed to steer their own learning in self-directed tasks.

And-ra-gog-i-cal approach – 'learner-led'

The andragogical approach allows the learner more independence and to steer their own learning.

Most of their time would be spent in self-directed tasks that allow them the opportunity to make their own decisions on how to fulfil the desired learning outcomes. More emphasis is placed on what the learner is doing, for instance the process of learning, such as carrying out research, skills or tasks. As learners are self learning, they can ensure that they learn in the best way to suit them. Depending on your specialist subject, you may use mostly a pedagogical or andragogical approach, but a mix of both approaches is usually best.

Activity:

Which approach have you used or seen used mainly in your subject specialism?
How could you adapt a lesson to use the alternative approach?

Reflective activity:

Can you think of a learning environment you have been in where the approach was purely teacher centred? (Pedagogical).

Can you think of an environment where your learning was your own responsibility? (Andragogical).

What were the pros and cons of each situation?

Teaching and learning approaches – strengths and limitations

Unit 2: 1.2, 2.2

The following table describes a variety of teaching and learning approaches with their strengths and limitations. When deciding on the appropriate approaches, it is important to select those that will meet or can be adapted to meet individual, group and subject needs. Consider the level of knowledge and skill your learners already have and where they need to get to meet the requirements of the learning objectives and assessment criteria. Also consider the timing of your lessons, group size and which approaches will be actively engaging and stimulating, taking into account your learner's learning styles. The diversity (of background, knowledge, experience, skill) within the group can be used to the advantage of all and could influence your choice of teaching and learning approach greatly.

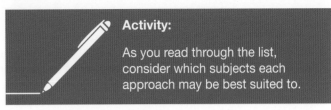

Activity:

As you read through the list, consider which subjects each approach may be best suited to.

Approaches strengths and limitations:

Teaching (T) / Learning (L) approach	Strengths and limitations	Andragogical &/ or Pedagogical
Explanation (T)	Gives a good level of detail. Delivered with the appropriate amount of information at the level of knowledge and language for the learners and the award. Explanation is the bedrock of teaching. Can be linked to a specific topic or criteria. If too much specialist language is used, or prior knowledge is presumed, or the explanation is insufficient, then learning may not be achieved.	Pedagogical
Presentation (T)	Delivering information. Can be informative, entertaining, motivating and interactive, using a variety of teaching aids and resources. Depending on the skills of the presenter e.g. monotone voice, uninterested in the material or poor presentation skills, could be disengaging and demotivating for learners.	Pedagogical
Questioning (T)	To clarify and confirm knowledge and understanding. When aimed at the right level for the group it is one of the best ways to teach and assess knowledge, include, involve, motivate and stimulate learners. Usually best delivered to the group as a whole. If the question is beyond the knowledge or language of the group or sometimes, if aimed at one individual, the learner does not know the answer, their confidence and motivation can be knocked.	Pedagogical
Shadowing (T/L)	A way of teaching or coaching one-to-one e.g. the learner learns by being alongside a colleague at work. This can be an efficient and very economical way of passing on a skill or information to a new member of staff. The success of this method may also be reliant on the pair's relationship and the ability to communicate with each other. Health and safety must be adhered to, especially in relation to equipment, machinery, vehicles etc. With shadowing, there is the potential risk that bad habits and attitudes may be passed on.	Andragogical & Pedagogical
Lecture (T)	A lecturer passing on information to many learners or colleagues, sometimes over a hundred in a lecture theatre. This can be a useful and cost-effective way to convey facts and theories to an audience on a similar level of knowledge e.g. at a conference. However, there is little opportunity for discussion as communication is usually one-way and there is no progressive check for understanding. Modern technology can now allow a greater opportunity for two-way communication, even discussion by messaging or texting the lecturer towards the end of the session.	Pedagogical

Tutorial (T/L)	A teacher with one learner, or a small group of learners. A tutorial enables two-way communication and can embrace a number of other methods of teaching but is essentially an andragogical approach where the learners come prepared to discuss the subject after completing their own research. This method can stretch both the learners and teachers, but is more expensive and needs time-management. Time may be wasted if learners are unprepared or the tutorial is not well-led.	Andragogical & Pedagogical
Demonstration (T)	Demonstrations are essential for teaching practical skills. Explain it and show it. Don't try to stretch powers of imagination by merely describing a skill. The skill must be practised by the learner for the session to be effective. A popular and effective method used in the military is **EDIP** – • **E**xplain the relevance and the main points of the skill or task using plain English, keeping it brief and simple. • **D**emonstrate the skill, explaining each step as you show them, making sure all learners can see. Then demonstrate again with a lesser explanation from a different angle • **I**mitate the demonstration by asking the learners to copy what you have shown them • **P**ractise the skill. The teacher provides coaching and gives constructive feedback to the learners, answering any questions they may have Without practise and coaching, learners may not acquire the skill, especially when it is a new skill or one that will be performed infrequently and learning cannot be checked.	Pedagogical EDIP Andragogical & Pedagogical
Practise (L)	Learning by doing. Opportunity to practise new skills with the appropriate resources is essential for learning and assessment. Ideally enough practise for the skill to become second nature. Learners may support, teach and assess one another and so build on these skills. Learning may not take place if practise is not coached and assessed. Poor demonstration or coaching skills of the teacher may lead to an insufficient standard of practise. Resources may not be fit-for-purpose. Can leave the learner without the necessary standard of skill.	Andragogical With coaching Andragogical & Pedagogical
Discussion (T/L)	Learner-centred. A well led discussion using resources (e.g. sticky notes) is a great way to use the diversity of experience, knowledge and ideas within the group. Discussion can constructively challenge values, beliefs and ways of doing things, out of which new ideas and understanding can be born. Can get side-tracked, or enthusiastic, out-spoken or dominant characters take over if not led well, so that quieter characters are inhibited and may not contribute. If prejudices or ideas from ignorance are voiced and not challenged/discussed appropriately, the group dynamic can suffer irreparably and some learners can be left unmotivated and demoralised.	Andragogical & Pedagogical
Case studies (L)	Learners are set an exercise individually or in groups that may be theory or practical based to stretch their minds and encourage team work and leadership skills. Allows learners to develop analytical and problem solving skills (sometimes very complex), allowing the learners to apply existing and new knowledge and skills. The case studies need to be relevant to the learner's own situation and well defined. Insufficient information or badly prepared tasks can lead to inappropriate results. Time management is necessary for completion and marking. The teacher must make sure all learners have reached the learning objectives.	Andragogical

Projects/ Research (L)	Learning by independent study. Can be done individually or as a group to cover different topics simultaneously in one lesson or over a period of weeks. Can be a useful time-saver and test initiative, imagination and entrepreneurial skills. Encourages ownership of work and sense of pride, developing planning and organisational skills, personal responsibility, team work and confidence. Gives a chance for more able learners to explore the topic further. One pitfall for projects set over time is that the group needs to organise itself and if a member does not do their fair share of the work they can let other learners down. If the task is assessed and graded and some learners have worked well and others not, that group may be marked lower. Another is that often one group only really learns about their topic to any depth and not about the others, so this is not ideal for important parts of a curriculum. It is best used with the groups working on the same topic and then feeding back to the whole group with discussion in class or perhaps through an IT portal like 'Moodle'.	Andragogical
Group work (L)	Learner-centred. When directed well, more interaction and communication within the group, resulting in teamwork and a positive group dynamic. Learners can be creative, learn to give constructive peer feedback and self-assess. Some learners may not be so involved resulting in others feeling like they are doing more work. If not well directed or designed to suit the needs of the group it may be dominated by certain learners. If there is a clash of personalities the work could go off on a tangent.	Andragogical
Blended Learning (L)	The term given to a formal programme of learning in which the learner learns through a mix of face-to-face instruction and online delivery of content. These elements allow learners some control over the time, place, and pace of the course. Blended learning provides the opportunity for the collection of data regarding the progress of a course and any differentiation in instruction and assessment, including the allocation of resources.	Andragogical & Pedagogical
Visits (T/L)	Experiential learning. This may be visiting a place, area of work, or equipment. All the senses are used and the place/staff/equipment become familiar, allaying any potential fears. Learning can be achieved and gain more meaning by being given a context and purpose. If the place/staff/equipment are unprepared, uninterested or not fit-for-purpose, any potential gain from the visit may not be achieved, or a negative impression being left and learners left determined to avoid the situation in the future.	Andragogical & Pedagogical

Activity:

Choose four of the following approaches most suitable for your subject specialism. Research them by asking colleagues and learners what their experiences are of them.

Assignments, drawing, e-learning, essays, exercise, film-clips, games, guest speakers, panel of experts, quizzes, readings, scenarios, seminars, simulation, tests, worksheets.

Activity:

List some attitudes, behaviours and teaching methods that you have found de-motivating in the past. List those that have really inspired and motivated you.

Reflective activity:

What effect did those positive and negative experiences have on your learning? Why do you think they were negative or positive? How did you feel when those experiences occurred? How long did they affect you for?

Activity:

Thinking about your subject specialism, outline an example session where you could use the **EDIP** method of teaching. What resources would you use? Whose teaching theory would apply to which resources? Which learning styles would each resource suit best?

Teaching techniques

Unit 2: 1.2, 2.2

Presentation skills

Visual aids and props are a useful way of adding to a lesson to emphasise certain points, add interest and make lessons more enjoyable. Visual aids and props will suit those learners who are more strongly visual and kinaesthetic (tactile, movement) learners. There are some golden rules when using these valuable tools:

Film clips and photographs

- Very useful as a teaching aid, but not a substitute for a live teacher.

- Use to enhance training, to make a point or bring information together.

- Keep the clip short, up to date and relevant, and always discuss it.

- Never use a film clip to cover a whole lesson and best not straight after lunch in a darkened room. Stay out of the way while your learners are watching so that you don't distract them – this is not a time to catch up on your text messages.

- Know your equipment and check it is working before the lesson.

Exhibits –

- Resist saying anything important whilst they are being circulated as the learners are busy looking at and handling the exhibit, not listening to you.

- Have enough samples for the group.

Flip charts, PowerPoint and Smartboards

- Use UPPER and lower case because BLOCK CAPITALS CAN BE MUCH HARDER TO READ, and use a font size large enough (36) for your learners to see clearly.

- Use a font that is easy to read, bold, plain and spaced well. Good examples are Arial, Gill Sans MT, Tahoma, Verdana, Helvetica, *Comic Sans* and Calibri. Serif or script fonts tend to be too fussy and difficult to read, for example Times New Roman and *Vivaldi*.

Keep presentation material as simple as possible, using 3 or 4 bullet points and colourful graphics (avoiding pale pastel colours). Wherever possible, use colour coding and colour association, for example blue for air or water, red for danger, love or blood. How things are projected onto a screen can be very different to how they appear on your computer screen or on a page, so experiment with different backgrounds and text colours on PowerPoint presentations and Smart-boards. It may be worth asking your learners which they prefer.

Flip charts can be seen as old fashioned, however, they can be a great way to create a mind map with your learners. It is very motivating when your answer or idea is right or good and it is used and written up. A good technique to use is known as the 'Hide and Reveal' technique where you reveal or write up one point a time. This prevents the learners reading ahead and embeds the information that is being discussed. This can be done with PowerPoint too. PowerPoint also allows for the previous point to be dimmed or 'greyed out'. Speak to the learners, not the screen or paper. When using flip charts ensure you have spare paper and check your pens work.

The general rule with all of these aids is to talk to your learners and not the screen, exhibit or flip chart.

The lighthouse technique

This is one of the most simple and effective ways to be inclusive in your teaching. Like a lighthouse, scan the group so that you have eye contact with all your learners throughout the lesson. Of course don't stare, as this would be unnerving. Simply ensure that you look at everyone so that they are all included in the lesson and motivated. This also helps to establish trust and to assess your group's understanding of what you are saying, or, if anyone has a question. It will take some practise and you may need to avoid the temptation to look/talk only at the learners who seem engaged and interested.

Body language has been an area of interest for many disciplines, for example anthropology, psychology, medicine and business. Your posture and manner will affect your group and theirs will affect you. However, don't have a fixed presumption about their stance, as there could be various reasons as to why they are sitting or standing that way. Some of the classic body signals and their meanings are:

Nodding their head – they agree with what you are saying or know it already

Frowning – they may not like, or are thinking about, what you are saying

Raising eyebrows – they are surprised by what you are saying

Questioning look – they may not have fully grasped what you are saying

No reaction at all – they may not be interested in what you are saying and don't want to make an issue of it

Looking away from you – they may disagree with what you are saying

Attention wandering – they may not be interested in what you are saying or you are taking too long to say it

Drumming fingers or tapping pen on table – they may be irritated by what you are saying

Constantly moving on their chair – they are perhaps annoyed or impatient with what you are saying

Moving or leaning away from you – they may disagree with your case and may not support it

Moving or leaning towards you – they may agree with your case and may support you

Arms folded – they may be closed-minded, feel like they already know what is being said or may not want to be in that particular lesson.

Activity:

Think of the body signals on page 45 and suggest some other reasons why learners may be behaving in those ways. Which postures could you adopt that would encourage a positive impact on your lesson?

Reflective activity:

Think about how you sit or stand as a learner and why. Observe the body language of your teacher and your peers. How do certain postures that you take or your teacher takes affect you? How do they affect the class atmosphere? When you plan your micro teach, think about how you will stand, sit and move around the room. What atmosphere do you want to create? How could you appear confident and professional without appearing distant?

Questioning techniques

Unit 2: 1.2, 2.2

"Questioning is an essential tool that effective teachers always carry with them"
Michael Clough, editor of Iowa Science Teachers Journal.

Asking the right sort of questions is an invaluable method of inclusive teaching and can be used to:

- promote thought in learners so that they are motivated to participate fully

- promote group activity, so team spirit is developed and the whole class remains interested

- promote a culture open to questioning, so that learners know that they can ask more questions to increase and deepen their knowledge

- test, assess and ensure learning takes place. Learners also find out how much they know already, leading to an increase in confidence and motivation

To be inclusive, address questions to the whole group when teaching, that way no one will be inhibited by being put on the spot or the fear of being so. The same goes for when learners have asked you a question; you will involve the group by giving the answer to them all. Remember that to be involved is to be motivated.

Types of questions

'Pose, prompt and pounce' is where the teacher sets a scenario and gives enough information before asking the question. This helps to give the learner confidence in finding and stating their answer, for example "When approaching a junction in your car, it is important to... take your foot off the accelerator and...?"

'Hobson's choice', 'yes or no', or 'right or wrong'. Closed questions are best avoided if possible as you run the risk of setting a learner up for a fall, for example. "Should you fertilise the ground for Lavender plants?" Sometimes this type of question is unavoidable, depending on the level of the learners and the course. You can set them up for a win by your facial expression, for example, smiling openly if the answer is yes and frowning if it's no. For learning to be at its most effective you should aim to ask open rather than closed questions.

Open questions, if they are asked well, allow a more complete answer as opposed to just yes or no, for example "What is your favourite childhood memory?" They also allow the learner to ask other questions to clarify the question and its context. Open questions often start with the words:

- what
- which
- why
- who
- how
- when

Leading questions are best avoided as the learner will almost always agree, for example "You agree with me don't you? If you do use them, set the learner up for a win, because if they've got it right it will boost their confidence.

Clarifying the question, being able to explain the question or putting it another way is a valuable skill. A key thing to remember is 'if you don't get the answer you want, you've asked a poor question.' Either the learners don't have enough information or knowledge to answer, which could be down to you, or the question is unclear or unreasonable, for example, asking them to state or explain something they have not yet covered. Remember, it is not clever to deliberately mislead the learner (no one likes to be humiliated).

Activity:

List five well structured questions that you can use in a lesson when teaching your specialist subject.

Learner answers

To teach and assess inclusively, allow learners to include aids and non-verbal communication to give their answers. Some learners will prefer to use their power of expression non-verbally, especially pertinent when considering disability, language or literacy challenges.

Learners need to know whether or not they have given the correct answer. Handling wrong answers takes skill and sensitivity – don't 'flatten' people and make them look small, their answers provide us with insight to how best we can adjust our teaching to meet their needs. It also be used to explain why the answer was incorrect, leading to the correct answer and so turning their initial answer into a positive for further learning. That way no one loses face.

"Through the art of thoughtful questioning teachers can extract not only factual information, but aid learners in: connecting concepts, making inferences, increasing awareness, encouraging creative and imaginative thought, aiding critical thinking processes, and generally helping learners explore deeper levels of knowing, thinking, and understanding."

(Reece, I. 2007)

Discussion

For a successful discussion or debate to take place, both sides must have knowledge of the subject being discussed. The discussion must also be led and kept relevant to the topic. As with the tutorial there is potential for time wasting and, if not managed well, not everyone having their say or partaking.

Humour

Learning should be enjoyable and the introduction of appropriate humour is a good thing. Even when the subject is serious there will be opportunities for lighter moments in all lessons. Light humour will help relax the learners and make the lesson more memorable. However, it is important to use humour that strengthens the subject, rather than introducing trivia as then the joke is remembered but not its significance.

"For the advice in a joke is sometimes more useful than the most serious teaching"
Balthasar Gracian, The Art of Worldly Wisdom

References and further information

Bloom, B.S. (1956) *Taxonomy of Educational Objectives*: Handbook 1, New York: Longman

Coffield, F., Moseley, D., Hall, E., Ecclestone, K. (2004). *Learning styles and pedagogy in post-16 learning. A systematic and critical review.* London: Learning and Skills Research Centre.

Gardner, H 1993 *Multiple Intelligences – the Theory in Practice.* New York: Basic Books

Kolb, D (1984). *Experiential learning: Experience as the source of learning and development.* Englewood Cliffs, NJ: Prentice-Hall.

Laird, D (1985) *Approaches to Training and Development*, Harlow, Addison Wesley

Maslow, A (1987) *Motivation and Personality* 3rd Edition. Harlow: Pearson

Peter, LJ and Hull, R (1969) *The Peter Principle: Why Things Always Go Wrong*. New York: William Morrow & Company, Inc.

Reece I, Walker S (2007) *Teaching, Training and Learning*, 6th Edition, Houghton-le-Spring: Business Education Publishers Ltd

Rogers CR, (1983) *Freedom to Learn for the 80s*, Columbos, OH:Merrill

Skinner BF (1974) *About Behaviorism*, San Fransisco, CA: Knopf

Vygotsky, L.S. (1978). *Mind and society: The development of higher psychological processes*. Cambridge, MA: Harvard University Press

Fleming, N. (2012). Introduction to Vark.

Websites

Honey, P and Mumford, A

Chapter 3
Inclusive teaching and learning in education and training

In this chapter we will discuss:

- Inclusive learning
- Communication skills
- Creating the best conditions for learning and motivation
- Learning disabilities: Dyslexia and Specific Learning Difficulties in adults
- Ways to embed functional and wider skills in the specialist area
- Record keeping and meeting the learners' and the organisation's needs

Chapter 3
Inclusive teaching and learning in education and training

Inclusive learning

Unit 1: 1.3, 1.4

Inclusive simply means to include everyone. In education, inclusive learning means that the teacher involves everyone in their group.

Throughout your teaching career and your subject specialism you will be introduced to new terminology. Every profession and specialism uses its own language, or if you like, jargon. Mostly this is helpful as it means that those 'in the know' can communicate quickly, easily and effectively. Problems occur when those who aren't 'in the know' need to be and are left behind or act without being fully informed. Also, the same abbreviations may be used by different fields but mean different things, for example; IFA = Irish Football Association; Independent Franchise Association; International Federation of Aromatherapists to name but a few. It is a teacher's job to introduce and explain specialist terminology, vocabulary and concepts using language that the learners will understand.

Four terms that are essential for teachers are:
Diverse – being different;
Equality – having equal rights;
Inclusive – being included;
Differentiate – to make different/distinguish between

Diversity – People are different from one another. We must recognise this in education and respect and value those differences in people, for example, their background, culture or age.

Equality – In education equality means that all learners have the same rights and value as each other, giving them an equal opportunity to learn.

Inclusivity – Being inclusive, including all components and people. In education being inclusive means that we involve all learners in relevant activities and do not exclude anyone, either directly or indirectly.

Differentiation – In education, differentiation means using a range of different approaches and resources to meet the needs of all learners in your group.

"Differentiation can be defined as an approach to teaching and learning that both recognises the individuality of learners and also informs ways of planning for learning and teaching that take these individualities into consideration."
(Tummons, 2010)

Teachers need to recognise that learners are different and that they have different backgrounds and needs (diversity), in order to include them all (inclusivity) and give them all an equal chance of learning (equality). Teachers need to use different teaching and learning approaches, materials and resources to help them learn (differentiation).

The Equality Act 2010 embeds these principles in law; in society, work and education.

Learners don't need a 'label' in order to be included – everyone needs to be involved, from the most able and quick at learning to those who find learning more challenging.

It is part of a teacher's role to embrace and encourage diversity and to promote an inclusive culture. This is achieved by treating all with equal respect and dignity and being non-judgemental, though, always exercising discernment. There is a huge difference between judgement and discernment. For example, judgement would state that someone is entirely bad for behaving badly (judgements tend to be 'black and white'), whereas discernment would say that the behaviour is unacceptable but would still recognise the worth of the person, seeing different aspects of them and the situation (i.e. would see 'the grey area').

Diversity is to be appreciated and is of value to your group. Your learners will learn from each other as well as you and vice versa. There are the obvious differences people have, for example, gender, race or physical ability. However there are less obvious and yet equally important aspects that make us who we are. For instance:

Educational – qualifications, work and life experience, skills, educational experiences.

Personality – levels of confidence, self-esteem and motivation, attitudes, learning styles, emotional intelligence and maturity, personal goals.

Incidental – personal commitments and dependents, available time, work life, IT skills and access, age, disability, talents.

Cultural – first language, multi-lingual, religion and philosophy, country or place of origin, social background, actual or perceived social status.

Communication skills

Good communication skills are essential to teaching, learning and an organisation's success. A teacher who mumbles, speaks in monotone or too quickly, or who does not repeat important points nor explain technical specialist terms will not be effective. Non-verbal communication should also be considered, for example a teacher's appearance and manner. Learners respond differently when being given information and listening is quite a skill in itself. Being distracted can mean that learners take in only part of what is being taught. Communication and therefore teaching will be more effective if we articulate clearly, stimulate the senses to suit all the learning styles, make the information relevant, meaningful and use repetition. Using these different approaches will enable the memory to respond positively.

Creating the best conditions for learning and motivation

Unit 1: 2.1 Unit 2: 2.1

Learners need to feel safe, comfortable and at ease to be able to learn. Simple things such as being in a well ventilated room with natural light, room layout, being warm enough and regular breaks all affect learning. These are basic needs which we sometimes take for granted and yet can be missed. Being uncomfortable physically, emotionally or psychologically is a real barrier to learning, for instance – being too cold or hot, noise, language difficulties or other barriers to communication, literacy difficulties, difficulties with others in the group, health problems or problems at home. Most of these are beyond your remit as a teacher, so you may want to refer the learner to another professional (see *Points of referral, page 20).*

Maslow's Hierarchy of Needs and Motivation

Abraham Maslow, a motivational psychologist, developed the Hierarchy of Needs model in 1940-50s America, and his Hierarchy of Needs theory is still popular today for understanding human motivation in any context; learning, business and personal. Maslow's Hierarchy of Needs was originally based in a business context and presented the idea that it is the responsibility of employers to provide a workplace environment that encourages and enables employees to fulfil their own unique potential (self-actualization). This basic premise has been adopted by academics in many fields such as teaching, medicine and sociology and the Hierarchy of Needs has been interpreted and adapted for their purposes. Once people's basic physical and psychological needs are met they are more motivated and able to learn.

Self-actualisation
- Be enthusiastic and supportive
- Encourage projects and plans
- Be positive about the future
- Promote optimism

Self Esteem (Pride)
- Encourage independence
- Praise where appropriate
- Welcome ideas
- Treat learners with dignity

Love and Belonging (Feeling accepted)
- Show that you care
- Promote interaction between students
- Promote cohesive class climate

Safety and Shelter (Safe from harm)
- Maintain confidentiality/privacy as necessary
- Treat learners fairly
- Observe and chart accurate information
- Follow safety rules when necessary

Physical (Comfort requirements)
- Provide adequate breaks
- Ensure comfort
- Arrange seats according to needs
- Be alert to heating and ventilation requirements

Adapted from "Study Guide for Health, Social Care and Support Workers". Beverly Robertson.

Motivating learners

All learners vary as to how motivated they are. Some learners are very self-led in their learning and others need more support and guidance. Some of your learners may have been told that they have to do your course and so are quite resistant to learning at first. Others may have sought out the course and have opted to do it themselves, so they are extremely motivated from the start. It is sensible for you to find out what motivates your learners as someone who wants to learn will learn more easily and quickly.

Being aware of the need to learn a new skill, procedure or do research will motivate learners. Having plenty of opportunities to practise and experiment, receiving positive and constructive feedback and reinforcement of the correct new skill will embed learning and motivate further. Of course there must be adequate, suitable materials and resources available for learners' use and practice, for example one computer per learner for an ICT course or one car for a driving lesson.

If you can show the need, relevance and benefits of learning on your course, you will engage and motivate your learners more easily. The teaching should be done using a level of language and skill familiar to the learners, suitable for their level and in ways that cater for their different learning styles. As a teacher, you can then gradually start introducing new information to stretch and further their knowledge and skills.

If you think of your experiences of being taught and consider things that have really put you off and de-motivated you, this may help you think of ways you can actively motivate your learners.

Activity:

Look at the learning needs of your group to whom you will be delivering your micro teaching session. Explain how you will engage and motivate your learners in your session.

Icebreakers

Unit 1: 2.1 Unit 2: 2.3

Icebreakers are an invaluable and inclusive way to encourage learners to talk to one another, get to know each other's names and encourage group coherence. It is also a good way for you to observe your learners and can form a good initial assessment. You may want to use icebreakers to see who is naturally comfortable speaking to others, who leads, who listens and includes others, and it can also help you gauge how motivated your learners are.

To break the ice, firstly introduce yourself so that your learners know who you are, whether or not you will be teaching them for the duration of the course, your expertise and your place within the organisation. There are a great many icebreakers available. Some good examples include:

- **The interview:** Ask your learners to talk in pairs and interview each other. Learners can then introduce one another to the rest of the group. The information presented could include the person's name, their occupation, reasons why they are taking the course, whether or not they've done a similar course before, and a hobby. This can be very nerve-racking experience for the learner when talking to the group, but it is a good way for you to assess which learners presenting comes naturally to, who is motivated and other personality traits within the group. This icebreaker can also be done if you are teaching one to one by giving the learner some general information about yourself.

- **Creating a diagram:** In small groups of three or four, ask your learners to create a diagram or map of a relevant subject in plasticine, for example the digestive system for a biology related session. Ask a spokesperson to describe the diagram to the rest of the group. This activity should give you some additional information about learning styles, team spirit, subject knowledge and attitudes.

If you are delivering a short course and time is limited it is enough to ask the learners to say their name, where they work, and ask if they have they done this course before. Sometimes employees are pressured to attend a course by their employer and as a result they may resent being there. You could simply add to the questions above, said in a light way "do you want to be here?' This is a really good way to break the ice and encourage openness and honesty, usually making people relax and laugh. It also shows that you empathise with your learners. This simple icebreaker is essentially a quick initial assessment and an opportunity for you to motivate your learners by showing them the benefit of being on your course.

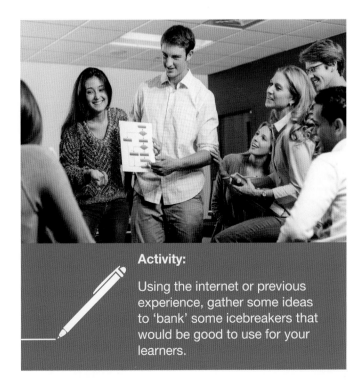

Activity:

Using the internet or previous experience, gather some ideas to 'bank' some icebreakers that would be good to use for your learners.

Group behaviour

Unit 2: 2.3, 2.4

People can behave very differently in groups compared to when they are on their own. Each person in a group will be affected by the group and often acquire a 'role'. You may notice, or have noticed that if a strong personality from the group is missing, or there is a change of venue, the dynamic changes. Most new groups of people go through a certain pattern of behaviour as the group forms. This is worth knowing so that you understand why the dynamic is changing and can encourage group coherence. It will also explain why the first day with a new group can be exhausting. Bruce Tuckman's (1965) widely used model of group development and behaviour states that the group evolves through five stages:

1. **Forming** – the 'getting to know you' stage. People are usually on their best behaviour. Some may be anxious about others in the group or the work ahead.

2. **Storming** – the 'it can't be done' stage, where clashes and disagreements can occur between members of the group, or, as often happens, there are some concerns about the teacher or the organisation.

3. **Norming** – the 'it can be done' stage where things settle down and the group becomes more cohesive and co-operative. The norms are established and the group bonds.

4. **Performing** – the 'doing it' stage where with the norms established, members feel safe to express their views and feel more enthusiastic about the tasks.

5. **Adjourning** (added in 1975) – is the 'separate but let's do it again' stage where the task or course is complete and the group separates. The members often feel that they want to keep in touch with each other.

Depending on the group's make up (for example the members may already know each other) it may not go through all five stages, but progress to the performing stage. However, it is best to be aware of the standard pattern of group behaviour and use this as a guide. When you first meet your learners, introduce yourself and ask them to introduce themselves and take part in an icebreaker. From then on, try to remember their names (not always possible with large groups). If remembering names isn't a talent you have, you may wish to ask them to wear a label with their name on it. This helps the learners to get to know each other's names too and helps to establish group coherence.

Ground rules

Unit 1: 2.1, 2.2 Unit 2: 2.4

Setting up ground rules at the start of a course is a great way to explore the diversity of the group, treat all with equal respect and bring everyone in, so exercising our guiding principles. Start by agreeing with the group a few basic rules about attendance and punctuality, acceptable behaviour, mobile phone use, breaks etc. You can then lead a discussion on your responsibilities, those of the learners and your expectations of the group. These can be reviewed as the group gets to know one another better. Some rules are non-negotiable of course and you may need to cover these in more detail, for example health and safety regulations or the organisation's own particular rules and procedures.

Adults are usually more motivated to learn, and so are willing to have an agreed set of ground rules so as to not waste time. However, if you are teaching professionals with a strong code of conduct and ethics already instilled, it could seem a little patronising. In this case, just agreeing start and finish times, who to contact if they're off-sick, switching phones off, etc would be sufficient. With groups where behaviour may be varied or more challenging, it's a good idea to let the whole group create the rules. This encourages learners to agree to them and motivates them to keep their own code especially if the rules are on show. Of course, you the teacher should stick to the rules too, showing mutual respect.

Having ground rules in place gives your learners firm boundaries to work within. For some learners this is more important than for others, particularly with those who have challenging behaviour. If the group have set the code and a learner breaks a ground rule, it is usually the other learners who reprimand them. Peer pressure is very effective in reinforcing the code.

Recognising, understanding and dealing with challenging behaviour

Unit 1: 1.4, 2.2 Unit 2: 2.3, 2.4, 4.1, 4.2

The following table shows examples of challenging behaviour, the motivations, the affects on the teacher and others and possible strategies to help change their behaviour.

The four main goals of disruptive behaviour	Learner's actions	What the learner is saying with their behaviour	How others feel (e.g. teacher / others in the group)	Learner's reaction to reprimand	Appropriate procedures	
					Preventive action	Consequence
Attention (to keep others busy with them)	Nuisance, show-off, clown, lazy. Puts others in their service. Pesters, whining, noisy, interrupting	"I only count when I'm being noticed or served." "I want you to notice me, do things for me, fuss over me." "I'm going to keep you busy."	Irritated, annoyed, thinks "they occupy too much of my time." Reminds often, coaxes. Delighted with 'good' learner, "I have to do it for them."	Temporarily stops disturbing action when given attention then repeats action.	Give lots of positive attention at more appropriate times. Make a contract. Look at your own behaviour and its effects on the learner and modify where necessary.	Ignore/walk away when attention is demanded. Follow through on contract and apply logical consequence. Avoid negative attention.
Power (seeks to be boss)	Does little or no work. Stubborn, argues, temper tantrums, tells lies, disobedient. Does the opposite of what they are told. Devious, bossy, uncooperative.	"I only count when I am dominating/when you do what I want you to do." "I want to be boss." "You can't make me do that." "You can't stop me."	Feels threatened or provoked. Thinks "they can't do this to me .... I'll make them do it." Determined to control the learner's behaviour. "I can't get them to."	Intensifies action when reprimanded. Learner wants to win, to be boss. Feels they have won when others get upset. Refuses to cooperate. Smiles to self.	Avoid power struggles by offering choices. Provide situations where learner can use power productively. State rules ahead of time. Mutual respect. Solicits learner's help.	Remain unemotional. Be firm without dominating. Remove yourself from the area. Act – don't talk. Provide for cooling period.
Revenge (wants and tries to get even)	Hurtful (physically or verbally). Defiant, sullen, negative attitude. Kicks, bites, scratches. Steals, sore loser, calls names, swears, destructive, vicious	"I can't be liked." "I don't have power, but I'll count if I hurt others as I am hurt by them." "I feel hurt and I'm going to pay you back."	Feel deeply hurt and angry. Thinks "how can they do this to me." Dislikes learner. Retaliates.	Wants to get even, retaliates. Aims to be disliked. Hurts others.	Take time and effort to help learner. Enlist the aid of a friend of the learner. Encouragement from the group. Build upon learner's strengths.	Avoid retaliation. Do the unexpected. Remove yourself from the conflict. Maintain order with a minimum of restraint. For damage/ stealing ensure reparation. Avoid moralising.
Display of inadequacy (wants to be left alone)	A loner. Feels hopeless; 'stupid' actions. Feels inferior. Gives up easily. Rarely participates. Doesn't try.	"I can't do anything right so I won't do anything at all." "I am no good, so leave me alone." "I give up."	Feels extremely helpless and discouraged. Thinks "I give up – I don't know what to do anymore." Despair. Throws up hands.	Retreats further. Becomes more passive. No reaction, little if any eye contact.	Encourage learner to try...minimise mistakes. Have faith in the learner's ability. Be approachable (on their side). Trust with small responsibilities. Avoid giving choices initially. Demonstrate the desired behaviour.	Don't expect immediate results. Emphasise success. Give recognition at unexpected times.

Learning difficulties: Dyslexia and specific learning difficulties in adults

Unit 1: 1.4 Unit 2: 1.1, 2.1, 2.2

Specific Learning Difficulties (SpLDs), or some prefer 'differences', are as common as around one in seven people, so it is likely that you would have someone with an SpLD within your group. SpLDs are a family of related conditions which together affect around 15% of people to some extent. They are neurological in origin and usually hereditary. The likelihood of a person having any of the SpLDs is unaffected by social class, race, or intelligence. The broader term Learning Difficulties (LD's) is more generalised and includes conditions that do affect intelligence. SpLDs interfere with the way information is learned, so as teachers it is important to at least know the basics of the most common conditions.

Dyslexia is an information processing problem, thought to affect around 10% of the population, 4% severely. It is the most common of the SpLDs, characteristically presenting as weakness with written language. Also significantly affected are short term memory, speed of information processing, sequencing ability, organisational skills, mathematics, language and speech.

For more detailed information on dyslexia, please go to the British Dyslexia Association (BDA) website.

Dyspraxia is a developmental coordination disorder (DCD). It is a common disorder affecting fine and/or gross motor coordination in children and adults, often coupled with the difficulties consistent with Dyslexia. Individuals may vary in how their difficulties present, for example typing, speech, riding a bike or catching a ball. These may change in time with life experiences and demands.

Attention Deficit Hyperactivity Disorder (ADHD) and **Attention Deficit Disorder (ADD)** cause lack of attention, restlessness and erratic, impulsive behaviour which is often inappropriate and sometimes aggressive. Individuals with ADD do not display hyperactivity but have similar problems with attention and remaining focused.

Autism is neurological disorder where thinking is often inflexible and routines are heavily relied upon. People with autism tend to dislike change, excitement, or excessive movement around them. They often lack social and communication skills. It is wise to adopt a calm even approach here.

Asperger Syndrome is one of the autistic spectrum disorders. It is classified as a developmental disorder that affects how the brain processes information. People with Asperger Syndrome have a wide range of strengths, weaknesses, skills and difficulties. Some may experience a range of problems, including difficulties in forming friendships and relationships, communication difficulties (such as a tendency to take things literally), and an inability to understand social rules and body language. They may also experience difficulties in finding a suitable job. Training and experience can help to build coping skills.

Meares Irlen Syndrome is a visual perceptual problem, which can affect up to 20% of the population. If undetected and unassisted it can result in underachievement in school and at work, as well as causing physical discomfort such as headaches, migraine, eyestrain, stress and fatigue. It affects mainly reading and writing based activities but also for some people, concentration, balance, coordination and depth perception.

More than any other learning difficulty, the likelihood is that you will encounter learners with dyslexia or Meares Irlen Syndrome at some point in your teaching career.

Memory in Dyslexia

Short Term Memory (STM) deficit is a huge problem for people with dyslexia. A non-dyslexic person can hold on average seven 'chunks' of information in their STM. A person with dyslexia can hold on average only five. Coupled with this disadvantage is the fact that people with dyslexia tend to have difficulty 'chunking' or connecting information effectively. The non-dyslexic person can build on huge amounts of information to each chunk but the dyslexic person finds this more difficult. Long Term Memory (LTM) is largely unaffected by dyslexia but it takes longer to recall the information. It is important to note that once recalled, the information is just as accurate.

How can we enhance the learning process and memory for a learner with dyslexia or another SpLD?

Making a good initial assessment will benefit all learners and help to guide your teaching approach. As in all good teaching, using a variety of teaching methods to engage as many learning styles as possible and well chosen resources are key – course books, demonstrations and coaching learners through practise, games, role play, stories/real experiences and mnemonics (which are devices that assist the memory) such as colour association, acronyms, images and mind maps. These presentation skills and memory aids will be described in more detail in the next chapter. Courses that are fun and interesting are memorable courses. Being approachable and putting people at ease enables learners to feel comfortable and feel more able to ask questions or seek help.

As a teacher, for various reasons you may not be aware of learners with an SpLD within your group. Teaching inclusively and using a multisensory approach to your teaching will benefit all learners.

Things we cannot help, though, are the characteristic 'bad' days for those with SpLDs. We all have our bad days when information doesn't seem to sink into our heads but for those with SpLDs, these are far more pronounced and frequent. The challenge is to think of more ways to involve our learners, for example, recapping with mind maps drawn by them (people with SpLDs are often very creative), or using patterns of movements and actions with various scenarios, for instance, look, mirror, signal when driving, to help the learners revise. Finally always be aware, as far as you can be, of your learners and their individual needs. The best way to find out is through whatever form of initial assessment you and your organisation carry out. This may be an application form or induction period. (see Chapter 5)

Peripatetic = travel around – to teach at different venues

If you teach peripatetically and perhaps short courses for many customers in the business sector, the question of needing learning support is not always asked of the learners and when it is, the information may not reach the teacher. So an initial assessment may simply be you asking the learners to let you know if they have any particular learning needs at the beginning of the course. Ask them to let you know at the break so they can let you know discreetly. Don't forget if you feel a learner's needs are beyond your professional remit, you should refer them on to another specialist (see *Points of referral, page 20*).

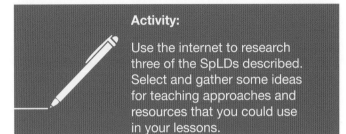

Activity:

Use the internet to research three of the SpLDs described. Select and gather some ideas for teaching approaches and resources that you could use in your lessons.

Reflective activity:

What experiences do you have of people with an SpLD? Have you found yourself being impatient with someone if they couldn't recall something quickly? Do you have an SpLD and have you received impatient attitudes? How could you ensure that you support someone with an SpLD in the learning environment? Why is this important?

Ways to embed functional and wider skills in the specialist area

Unit 2: 1.3

A skill is the ability to do something well, usually through practice and effort. You may have specialist skills you need in your area of training, for example developing senses of smell and taste for cooking or wine tasting, fine manual skills for engineering or carpentry.

There are however basic skills that are essential for modern life. These are;

- **English** (communication, speaking, reading and writing)

- **Mathematics** (using numbers)

- **ICT** (Information and Communications Technology).

In education these are referred to as functional skills (or basic skills, core skills, key skills, in the past).

Wider skills (or soft skills) are those that will improve learning and performance, for example time management, working with others (team work) and problem solving. These are all transferable skills and wherever possible should be developed and incorporated into your teaching. Teachers can demonstrate the importance of functional skills by showing how they are used within their specialised area, and embed them by giving their learners plenty of practice in using these skills. It can be done subtly so that the learners don't realise that they are developing these skills.

Examples include: Taking part in discussion or responding to direct questions (relates directly to the Adult Literacy Curriculum). Any written notes or assignments obviously fall within the reading and writing section. Timing an event or process could also be highlighted as embedding numeracy skills.

"Functional skills provide learners with the essential knowledge, skills and understanding that will enable them to operate confidently, effectively and independently in life and at work. Individuals of any age who possess these skills will be able to participate and progress in education, training and employment as well as develop and secure the broader range of aptitudes, attitudes and behaviours that will enable them to make a positive contribution to the environment in which they live and work".

(Functional skills update 2, QCA, 2005)

Activity:

What activities can you give your learners to embed their reading and writing skills?
Which subjects in your specialist area lend themselves easily to include numeracy and how would you teach them?
What activities can you ask your learners to carry out using ICT?
Identify the wider skills needed in your subject specialism. How might you embed these skills into your teaching?

Record keeping and meeting the learners' and the organisation's needs

Records help to build a picture of our learners. Records on attendance, progress and final results are not only important for each individual learner as evidence of their own achievements but for the teacher and organisation too, as they can inform you and your colleagues (if they are teaching the same learners) of any issues, for example, patterns of attendance or behaviour that highlight the need for support for that learner. Other recorded data is useful to inform equality and diversity and health and safety policies, including dispute and complaints procedures (for standardisation and quality assurance) and internal and external auditing. Evaluation of these records helps to design courses to better suit the learners' and organisation's needs and whether or not a course should continue to run.

Standardisation – the process that ensures that all teachers and assessors deliver the same information and evidence in the same way and to the same standards.

References and further information

Crisfield J. (ed) (1996) *The Dyslexia Handbook*. BDA Reading UK.

Miles Prof. TR 1993 *Dyslexia: The Pattern of Difficulties* (2nd Ed) London: Whurr

Robertson, B. 1992 *Study Guide for Health, Social Care and Support Workers*: Level 2 Second Edition Spokane WA: First Class Books

Tummons, J (2010) *Becoming a Professional Tutor in the Lifelong Learning Sector,* 2nd Edition. Exeter. Learning Matters

Articles

Tuckman, Bruce (1965). "Developmental sequence in small groups". Psychological Bulletin 63 (6): 384–99. doi:10.1037/h0022100. PMID 14314073. Retrieved 2008-11-10. "Reprinted with permission in Group Facilitation, Spring 2001"

Websites

British Dyslexia Association

Dyspraxia Foundation

Department for Education

The Higher Education Academy

Irlen UK

Interviews

Barron A. Specialist Tutor for East Durham and Houghall Community College. (Interview June 2013 and Course materials) Honey, P and Mumford, A

Chapter 4
Planning and preparing your lessons

In this chapter we will discuss:

- Planning and preparation
- Schemes of work
- Lesson plans
- Aims and objectives
- Planning the content and structure of your lesson in simple steps
- Writing up your lesson plans
- Energisers
- Selecting your resources
- Being prepared – things to consider
- Room layout
- Reviewing and justifying your choice of resources
- Record keeping and planning

Chapter 4

Planning and preparing your lessons

Planning and preparation

Unit 2: 2.2, 3.1, 3.2

> "Plans are of little importance,
> but planning is essential!"
>
> *Winston Churchill*

Planning and preparation are essential in teaching, as in most walks of life. Being prepared will help you to feel more positive, in control and relaxed while teaching, leaving room for some spontaneity and enabling you to adapt to unexpected situations should they occur.

Time management skills are also essential in teaching. Of course you need to be at your venue in good time to set the room up and prepare to welcome your learners but it is worth remembering that your time and that of your learners is valuable and needs to be respected, so not to over run lessons, etc. Be proactive, as good time management will help you to measure the progress towards your goals for the course and those of your learners. Timing is a skill which will develop more as you practice. It certainly helps to ensure the lesson and overall course goes well.

Planning your lesson will give you a really good perspective of how the lesson will flow, so that even if you get side tracked you can adapt and stick to your timing. Of course a clock is essential too and best if visible to the teacher but not the learners.

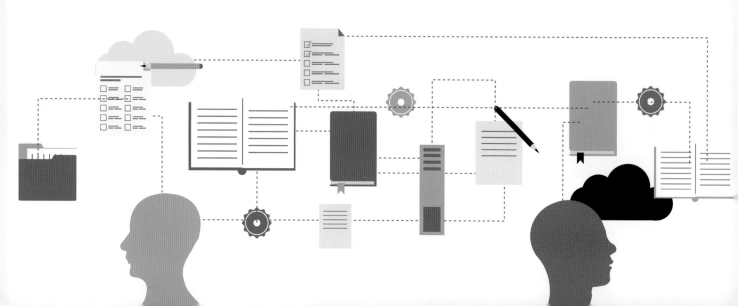

Activity:

What measures could you put into place at the planning stage that would help to ensure that you adhere to your timings as much as possible?

Reflective activity:

Think of a meeting or lesson you have led that was arranged at short notice with no time for you to prepare. What came out of that lesson that you felt was negative? What came out of that lesson that you felt was positive? What would you conclude from this experience?

When you have gained your Level 3 Award in Education and Training you will have to prepare your lessons carefully and thoroughly. You may also be required to write your own lesson plans. Perhaps it is more likely that you'll be using ones already prepared by your organisation. But as you progress through your teaching career you will certainly be designing and writing your own lesson plans, if not a whole course at some point. The following information is aimed at helping you write your lesson plan for your microteaching lesson (on which you will be assessed) but also to be a good grounding for your further progression later.

You will need to plan for the short term, medium term and long term:

Short term planning: Individual lesson plans.

Medium term planning: The units of the course or long-term plan, broken down into manageable sections.

Long term planning: An overview of the whole course including objectives and assessment, this is often called a *Scheme of Work*.

It is helpful when planning your courses to start with the long term schemes of work and work towards the individual lesson plans.

Schemes of work

A scheme of work is a medium to long term plan, sometimes referred to as an overview or a learning programme. It is a logical plan of learning through a whole course or one unit of a qualification, in which the overall objectives are clearly stated.

Some schemes of work include a basic skeletal lesson plan for each lesson. Experienced teachers may find that these give enough information and can work from these well. Another scheme of work includes creating detailed individual lesson plans for the whole programme of learning. When buying schemes of work and lesson plans from other organisations or awarding organisations, always check what information they actually include.

You may use a standardised scheme of work created by you and your colleagues. This is a good idea as it helps to ensure that you all teach the same material to the same standard (standardisation) and if the learners have a change of teacher, everyone knows which stage of the programme the learners are at. You may need to create your own scheme of work, for which you will need the course learning criteria, that is the specific objectives that dictate the content of the course mapped out by the awarding organisation.

If you are teaching a non-accredited programme, you will need to develop your own programme content and decide on the most suitable modes of delivery and assessment, and resources needed to meet the requirements of your learners.

For short courses, perhaps only a few hours in length, it may not be necessary to have a long term and medium term plan, you may just require the overview and the lesson plans. For longer courses, medium term planning will be required to break the overview into more manageable chunks from which you can write your lesson plans.

Scheme of Work / Overview

Teacher:

Course		Group		Duration From – To	
No of Sessions		Delivery Hours		Venue	
Aim of course					

Time	Main objectives (Learning outcomes)	Activities and resources Note embedded functional skills	Assessment method

Lesson plans

A lesson usually consists of three main sections; a beginning, a middle and an end.

In the beginning, introduce the subject and share with the learners what they will learn from that lesson – these are called the aims. Learners need to know why you are talking about a particular subject, why they have been asked to do something and what they'll need to remember from the lesson. If you do not do this and put the lesson into perspective, it will not work and can create anxiety or irritation which will block learning. This is true also for a lesson that just stops rather than reaching a final conclusion. It is important therefore to ensure that all lessons have all three sections.

The introduction is an overview of the lesson stating the aims and objectives, the expected outcomes, what activities will be included and how learning will be assessed. In the planning stages, this will help you identify the teaching and learning methods you choose as best for your lesson and learners. Link the information to any other relevant lessons and briefly recap the learning. Questioning is particularly useful here to assess the knowledge and previous experiences of the learners and to assess their knowledge from previous lessons.

The middle or development phase is the section used to introduce new concepts or develop existing knowledge to achieve the aims of the lesson. Use a variety of teaching and learning strategies to involve your learners and enable them to use their preferred learning styles whilst enhancing their weaker styles.

The end or conclusion draws together the objectives, concludes the lesson and assesses how the lesson has gone. Before the lesson finishes, review the lesson, give the learners feedback and allow them to feedback to you so you can assess if the lesson aims were achieved or require further development next time. Bearing in mind that we remember things for longer when they are relevant and useful, this is a great opportunity to link the lesson to the overall plan, the other things the learners may be studying and the next lesson. Outline any work that the learners will need to do to follow up this lesson, and how they can prepare for the next lesson.

When planning a lesson, remember to use a variety of resources and teaching and learning methods so that all your learners get maximum value from the lesson. In Chapter 2 we saw how people differ in their response to information and that we all have favoured learning styles. It is sensible to think about learners as individuals with their own needs and strengths and to present information in a variety of ways. Do this and the group will enjoy your lessons and get the maximum from them.

Your lessons may be delivered in a number of different ways; one-to-one, small or large groups. You may want your learners to learn by working on their own or as part of a team. Where possible you should vary the way in which you ask your learners to work to appeal to all different types of learners.

Aims and objectives

Aim – a broad statement of what learners will achieve from the lesson or course.

Objectives – are the stated detail of what is to be learned. They are written in a way that can be measured and specific, so that they can be assessed easily.

An aim or objective is simply what you want your learners to have achieved by the end of the lesson. Aims are the overall goal of the lesson, for example the learner will know how to change a carburettor on a car. Objectives and sub-objectives give more detail by giving the step-by-step sections of the lesson, for example 1) The learner can identify a carburettor, 2) The learner can demonstrate how to remove the carburettor, etc.

Identifying and stating your objectives clearly will provide a sound basis for selecting or designing your lesson content, organising learner activity and how best to evaluate and assess the success of the lesson.

An objective should achieve an observable and permanent change in behaviour (for example a new skill) and learning.

Objectives must be **SMART**

 Specific – clearly defined.

 Measurable – can be reliably tested.

 Achievable – possible.

 Realistic – relevant to the aims of the lesson.

Time bound – enough time to achieve the aims.

A **SMART** objective will tell the teacher and learner what they are expected to achieve in the lesson and how, to what standard and under what conditions. This is very useful when thinking about how to assess learners' progress too.

A **SMART** objective is a clear statement in behavioural terms, that is, what the learner is required to do. To be clear, the wording must not be open to misinterpretation (as far as is possible).

The following words are tempting to use but are not measurable and are open to misinterpretation:

Appreciate, be aware of, know, learn, listen, understand.

In Chapter 2 we discussed Bloom's Taxonomy of Learning (1956). Being aware of levels of learning and understanding will help you plan your sessions and write your objectives at the right level. Ask yourself how deeply do the learners need to know the subject? Or, how well do they need to be able to perform the skill? How complex is it? Do they simply need to state or copy something or get to a level where they can create, critique and problem solve?

Using both Bloom's and Anderson and Krathwohl's (2001) descriptors, the following table shows verbs that can be used with each level of learning from low to high level. These will help you to choose the right verb and level for your sessions.

Knowledge/Remember:
copy; draw; label; recognise; recite; repeat; show; state; use; weigh; write.

Comprehension/Understanding:
define; design; discuss; estimate; explain; identify; perform.

Application/Applying:
apply; build; change; divide; illustrate; interpret; modify; organise; solve; use.

Analysis/Analysing:
adapt; analyse; compare and contrast; categorise; integrate; modify.

Synthesis/Evaluating:
compose; summarise; structure; construct; organise.

Evaluation/Creating: complete;
compose; create; critique; discuss; evaluate; design; devise; justify.

Reflective activity:

How would these words help you to plan the assessment of your learners to the required level?

Activity:

Write out the aims and objectives of your microteaching session using appropriate words from the list above. (Remember to consider the level of knowledge or skill you want your learners to have).

Planning the content and structure of your lesson in simple steps

It is worth asking yourself some simple questions when planning a lesson:

- What background knowledge and experience do the learners need?

- Are the objectives clear? What do the learners need to know or be able to do by the end of the lesson?

- What are the principal step by step activities of the lesson? What is the most logical order for the information?

- Are the priorities of the subject matter clear, that is which parts are a 'must know', a 'should know' or simply a 'nice to know'? (You might want to cut out the 'nice to knows' if you are short of time)

- Which are the most appropriate teaching and learning methods to use?

- Does it cater for as many learning styles as possible?

- Which are the best resources to use?

- How will I embed functional and wider skills?

- What is the best method of assessing learning during and at the end of this lesson?

- Do any of my learners need resources to be adapted?

- Is the venue suitable and are the working conditions conducive to teaching and learning?

Properly prepared and planned lessons eliminate the risk of gaps in knowledge.

Writing up your lesson plans

There are many different formats for lesson plans. Your organisation may already have a template which you will have to use. Whichever you use, lesson plans must state the lesson title, its aims and objectives, the resources to be used, what prior learning is required of the learners, the maximum number of learners in the group and the timing of the lesson. They will sometimes also note the time, date and venue of the lesson.

Lesson Plan

Course		Trainer		Room	
Lesson		Date/time		Duration	
Aim					

Timing	Objectives (Learning outcomes)	Resources Note examples of differentiation	Trainer activities	Learner activities **VARK** Note use of functional skills	Assessment method Note examples of differentiation

Energisers

Unit 2: 2.1, 2.3, 2.4

"Spontaneity is one of the joys of existence, especially if you prepare for it in advance!"

Alan Dean Foster, Nor Crystal Tears

Similar to icebreakers, energisers are enjoyable activities that help to refresh people, particularly at the end of the morning, just after lunch or towards the end of the day when energy levels fall and people's attention wanders. A good energiser will do more than just wake people up, it can help learners get to know each other better, break down barriers and bring people from different backgrounds together.

Select energisers carefully, taking into account your learners' culture, gender, ability and any disabilities. Avoid situations that may not be appropriate for the particular mix of learners. If people have disabilities that prevent them from joining in, include them by asking them to give the directions or act as umpires or supervisors.

Begin with gentle, less energetic energisers for those unfamiliar with them and try joining in yourself to be part of the group. Respect those who really do not want to take part. Parts of your course may lend themselves well to an active kinaesthetic lesson and these will work really well as energisers. Even a serious subject will have its lighter side and will help lift the mood and remotivate your learners.

Regular breaks are important too, as they can give learners time and space to think and process the lesson. Many a good question or discussion is conceived in the break out session or informal break.

Activity:

Research energisers and create a collection suitable for your specialist area and work environment.

Selecting your resources

Resources are the equipment you will need to teach and assess that lesson, for example books, handouts or computers. They should be of a high quality and meet the needs of the lesson and the learners. Always ensure you have enough of each resource for your group.

Some resources are essential. For experiential learning to take place, you will need to have sufficient and relevant equipment for the group. For an IT group, for example, one computer per learner is necessary or, for a flying course, the learners and teachers need access to flight simulators and eventually a plane. Ensuring that learners practise with real or simulated equipment reinforces the learning on which they can reflect. Other essential resources might be course books, handouts and assessment papers. When designing written resources remember the presentation skills described in Chapter 2. Also, include your name, your organisation's name and the course title to show the document's origin.

Other resources supplement your teaching method and may add a different 'take' to the subject, for example 'sticky notes' on which learners can write ideas or prioritise aspects of the lesson, flip chart stand, paper and pens, laptop, projector, screen and icebreaker essentials. You may need to differentiate some resources to meet the needs of some learners. Ensure that the resources you select appeal to a wide variety of learning styles.

When preparing for a lesson, consider the policies of your organisation too and how they apply to you and your learners. You also need to consider issues relating to health and safety in the classroom or training environment and current regional and national standards. This is especially important in areas such as the military, construction industry or hospitality.

It's useful to introduce the learners to the resources just before you or they are going to use them, otherwise they may be distracted by them or read ahead. If someone is reading they are not watching and listening and so will miss important information. Ensure you have spares, for example, bulbs for your projector, pens for flip chart or chemicals for a chemistry experiment. Have all your resources prepared and in place before you start your lesson to avoid feeling rushed and unprepared.

Being prepared – things to consider

You may teach within a college, university, workplace or peripatetically, that is travelling to different venues or some other specific environment.

The following are some important things to help you prepare for different venues, particularly if you are peripatetic:

The venue:

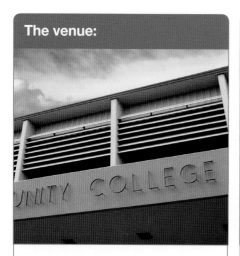

- is it the customer's premises or a hired venue?
- location and accurate address
- contact name, address and number of the company and their venue if they are different
- is there a key holder or caretaker to open up and lock up?
- security
- travel directions for the learners
- parking information
- building entrance and exits
- start and end times
- health and safety policy
- fire exit and meeting points
- smoking policy
- toilet facilities
- refreshments and meal provision
- is there noise pollution?

The learners:

- who are they?
- qualifications and occupations
- number of enrolled learners
- joining instructions
- course start and end times
- pre-course information
- prior knowledge
- special needs
- appropriate dress

Venue, room and facilities:

- room size and layout
- heating and lighting
- tables and seating
- equipment available and power sockets
- stationery
- facilities
- disabled access

Room layout

It is fairly obvious that if your teaching specialism has a strong practical bias, the need for the right equipment and the right environment is paramount to a successful lesson and assessment. You will often need a bigger room than when teaching a theoretical subject that does not require the learners to leave their chairs. Unfortunately, these things are not always obvious or available in the venues you may be required to use. It is therefore an essential part of planning your lessons to make it very clear in your communications with your client and the organisations in which you work and teach. It is helpful to spell out how much space and what equipment is required for your subject specialism for both you and your learners, for example, a chair per learner, working stations, tables or computer stations,

flip chart stand, projection equipment, extension leads or power points. It is also wise to let the venue know if you need disabled access or any other specialist equipment. By doing this you can ensure an inclusive environment and suitable learning aids for all of your learners. Send your joining instructions to each learner, or, ask their organisation to distribute them with details of the course.

Of course, your teaching environment could be anywhere such as a car, outside, a church hall or a specially designed classroom. If you are teaching indoors, how your room is set out and the pattern in which you sit your learners will greatly influence the dynamic of the group and the success in effectively teaching the learning objectives.

Example room layouts

It is important to make sure the space is tidy, well lit, a comfortable temperature and adequately ventilated. Some venues will have fixed furniture but wherever possible arrange the seating in the most suitable way for that particular lesson. Here are a few layouts:

Activity:

List examples of where each of the room layouts may be suitable for your subject specialism. Are there any room layouts which would never be suitable and why?

Traditional classroom: One or two learners at each desk and the desks in rows. This style is best for teaching theoretical subjects where no group work is required. All the learners will be able to see the teacher and any resources they are using, but communication is hindered here as the teacher is usually at the front. The teacher would need good voice projection or a microphone. Desks and tables can have a barrier effect, so it is good for the teacher to walk in between the desks and be closer to all the learners at some point in the lesson.

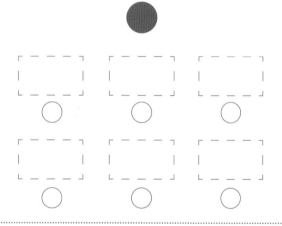

Lecture style: As above but without the desks. This allows for more seating, so good for larger numbers of people. Ideally the chairs would have a specially designed arm on which learners can lean to write notes, however, bear in mind left-handed learners. In specially designed lecture theatres the support space must take into consideration both the set up and use of audio-visual equipment, access for the disabled, layout of the instructor's materials, circulation space and empty floor space needed to keep learners from being seated too close to a chalkboard, projection screen, or video monitor. It goes without saying though, the larger the number of learners, the less opportunity for two-way communication with and assessment by the lecturer

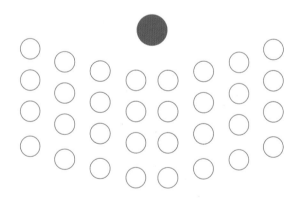

Boardroom style: Here learners and teacher are seated around one large table. This style is very good for lessons based on discussion and group work where the resources are on the table. It works best if the teacher is at the table with the learners, leading and chairing the discussion or activities. The setup here allows for all to have their say. This will not work if the teacher and resources are behind any of the learners.

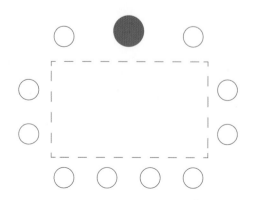

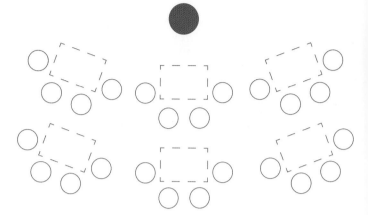

Cabaret style: This is excellent for a variety of lessons. Tables are set out as in a café but with only one half of each table occupied so that no one has their back to the teacher. It enables the learners to see the teacher and equipment and allows a larger group to work in their smaller 'table' groups for parts of the lesson.

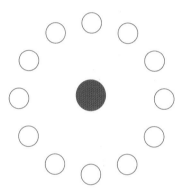

Circle: Very good for a lesson where the group need to feel safe as there are no barriers in between (e.g. no tables). It allows everyone to see each other and have their say. This setup can be a little too intimate for some until the dynamics settle.

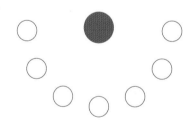

Semi-circle: This works really well for small to medium sized groups and lessons that have both theory and a strong practical element where demonstrations are necessary, especially floor work. Tables or desks would inhibit the view and act as a barrier. If the learners don't know each other (and especially if it's a short course), it helps to tighten the semi-circle so they can exchange eye-contact and cohere as a group. If they know each other well and there is distracting conversation between them, open the semi-circle so it's almost a straight line. This prevents eye contact and encourages them to focus on the teacher in front of them.

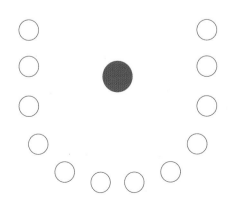

Horseshoe or U-shape: The U-shape works very well for larger groups, allowing discussion including the teacher. It also lends itself well to pair work but not small group work. Usually there would be tables too, so the U-shape is great for lessons that involve tabletop resources but not so good for floor demonstrations.

Reviewing and justifying your choice of resources

When using resources we need to reflect on:

- Did they do what we wanted them to do?
- Did they make an impact?
- Did they stimulate learning?
- Would we use the same resources again?
- Do we need to change them for next time?
- Were the resources inclusive to all learners?

Activity:

Using a suitable template, complete your lesson plan for your micro-teach lesson.

Reflective activity:

Do your choices of teaching and learning approaches and resources include all learners? How have you incorporated all your learners' needs? How did you differentiate your approaches and resources to ensure that you included everyone? Discuss this with your teacher; you may need to revise your lesson plan.

Reflective activity 2:

After your microteaching lesson reflect on your use of resources. Did they do what you wanted them to do? Did they add anything to the lesson? Would you use them again? Would you need to adapt them for next time or for certain learners?

Record keeping and planning

As we have seen throughout, keeping records is essential at every stage of planning, teaching and assessing. It will be useful for you to keep a 'course file', in which you can have all of your necessary documents; the course syllabus, schemes of work, lesson plans, handouts, assignments, activities etc. Many organisations use a standard format for keeping records; this is usually the case with class registers and learner grades. 'Learner files' are also very useful and contain the learner's application forms, interview notes, initial assessments, action plans, referral notes, tutorial notes, review notes and assessment records. You must be aware of confidentiality and the rules of the Data Protection Act when carrying around and dealing with such personal and sensitive information.

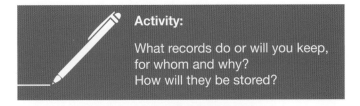

Activity:

What records do or will you keep, for whom and why?
How will they be stored?

Reflective activity:

How will the records you keep be useful to you? How will the records you keep help to make your teaching more effective?

References and further information

A 1999 study by David Fleming, now at Northumbria University, and John Storr, at Sheffield Hallam University, explored how learners and university Facility Managers (FMs) perceived the importance to the learning experience of various aspects of lecture theatre design.

Anderson, L.W. and Krathwohl, D.R. (eds.) (2001) A Taxonomy for Learning, Teaching and Assessing: A Revision of Bloom's Taxonomy of Educational Objectives New York: Longram.

Chapter 5
Understanding assessment in education and training

In this chapter we will discuss:

- Purpose and main types of assessment
- Assessment cycle
- Principles of assessment
- Planning assessments
- Main methods of assessment
- Principles of giving feedback
- Assessment decisions and feedback
- Peer feedback
- Self-assessment and self-evaluation
- Record keeping, evaluation and assessment
- Standardisation and quality assurance
- Completing your Level 3 Award in Education and Training and professional formation
- Continuing Professional Development (CPD)

Chapter 5
Understanding assessment in education and training

Purpose and main types of assessment

Unit 3: 1.1

"Assessment should be seen as an intrinsic part of the learning process rather than something which is just 'tacked on' at the end in order to get some marks".
Chris Rust – 2002

The purpose of assessment is to find out to what level, degree and depth of learning has taken place. Each stage of assessment enables planning of the next stage of learning and in turn, its assessment (see Assessment cycle). Planning and designing assessments is an integral part of your short, medium and long term planning.

Good quality assessment emphasises the most important aspects of the course, clarifying to the learners what to remember and develop in the long term and allow the opportunity for constructive critique and feedback, for both teacher and learner. When used well, this is invaluable and will motivate further learning and development.

A well designed assessment should be measurable and set at the right level so that personal and professional achievement can be acknowledged, especially when certification and qualifications are awarded.

The main types of assessment:

Initial assessment: Ideally an initial assessment takes place within the course application process. Its purpose is to see if the learner is suitable for the course they are enrolling on. Do they have previous knowledge or experience of the subject? Do they have any special needs? What are their learning styles? Will you need to adapt assessment methods for the learner? If you are teaching short courses and have little knowledge of your learners beforehand and initial assessment can be done by asking learners to introduce themselves to the group. Ask them to give their name, say whether or not they have done this sort of course before and to say what they hope to gain from it.

Ipsative assessment: Where the learner carries out ongoing comparisons and self-assessment of their own performance and development, with a set of standards on their own previous performance. This is mostly done autonomously, which takes self-awareness and honesty but ipsative assessment may also be guided by the teacher; for instance asking 'How do you feel you've done today? How did it compare with last time?'

Diagnostic assessment: A diagnostic assessment or skills test is designed to find out what level a learner is at in terms of a particular subject (often English, Mathematics or ICT, as a part of initial assessment), their abilities and if they have any learning needs. This form of assessment may be part of an actual diagnosis used by specialist tutors or educational psychologists to identify if a learner has, for example, Dyslexia or any learning needs. From these assessments the teacher gains an understanding of where the learner is at, how they might improve and what learning needs and resources they need to progress further.

Formative assessment: This is a continuous assessment throughout the course and an effective learning tool. Examples include; quizzes, practical skills tests, questioning sessions and mock exams. An important part of formative assessment is giving feedback to learners, verbally, written or both. Feedback will be discussed later in this chapter.

Summative assessment: A final, often more formal, assessment at the end of the course or lesson, such as a written exam, driving test, formal discussion, or an interview with the learner about their work.

Assessments can be either formal or informal

Formal assessments are often an obligatory part of a course going towards a final qualification. Formal assessments may be formative coursework, summative assignments or activities at the end of the course and must satisfy the course criteria set out in the course syllabus. The assessment and its feedback must be recorded accurately.

Informal assessments are not a set part of a course and the qualification achievement but are a very useful way to embed and gauge your learners' learning. Informal assessments can be made fun and are excellent for revision.

Assessment cycle

A useful tool to use when considering and undergoing the assessment process is the assessment cycle. Whichever subjects you teach, your assessment process will probably go through all the stages of the assessment cycle. Assessment is an ongoing process, so once the course and assessment has begun it is possible to start at any point in the cycle, continuously planning, assessing and reviewing until the learner has achieved their aim. The cycle will continue if they go on to prepare for and do another course.

Initial assessment – has your learner any previous knowledge or experience of the subject to be assessed? Recognition of Prior Learning (RPL) may take place here which can decide if the learner needs to take all parts of the course or if they already have credits that can go towards the final result. Find out if your learner has any special assessment requirements, their preferred learning styles, or any further training they may need.

Plan assessment – consider the types and methods of assessment suitable for the subject matter and for the learner. This can be decided with the learner and perhaps involve others, for example, colleagues or workplace supervisors. At this point it is useful to agree on the deadline and follow relevant guidelines.

Deliver assessment – carry out the assessment. Record keeping is essential here for both the assessor and the learner. The assessment method may be 'Assessor-led', for example observation or questioning, or 'Learner-led', for example, building a portfolio of assignments and evidence of learning.

Evaluate assessment and feedback – has the learner passed or is their pass referred? Constructive feedback is necessary and you may need to agree any further action required. A tracking sheet is a very useful tool in seeing what progress your learner has made towards each aspect of the qualification.

Review progress – you will review your learners' progress throughout the course until they complete their qualification. It may be necessary to adapt resources or teaching methods for certain learners in order to meet their needs.

Standardisation of assessments

Assessors make judgements about the competence of their learners by looking at the standards provided by their Awarding Organisation. They base their judgements on a variety of evidence provided by the learner. This may include observations of their performance in the workplace, products they have made or delivered, or written assignments but the key is to ensure that all assessors judge the same evidence in the same way and to the same standards. The IQA plays an important role in this. However, there may be more than one IQA and so decisions need to be consistent, reliable and through a standardised process.

The simplest means of completing a standardisation review is to collate copies of evidence available for the qualification from a range of assessors/IQAs. Each assessor makes a decision based on the evidence presented. It is also helpful to ask them to note any queries they may have, for example, further information needed or authentication of a piece of evidence. The process enables the programme team to check that each assessor is asking the right questions when looking at evidence as well as arriving at the correct decision.

Principles of assessment

Whichever method of assessment you use, you need to be sure it will be fit for purpose and measures exactly what you want it to measure and in the most pertinent and fitting way. It needs to be:

- **Authentic** – an assessment where the learner performs real life tasks that demonstrate a meaningful use of skills and knowledge. Assignments that are presented and marked must be the learners own work.

- **Current** – an assessment must measure skills and knowledge that are up to date in the learners' subject specialism. Is it benchmarked against industry standards? Does the evidence show that the learner can perform the skill while working?

- **Ethical** – the assessment is carried out with regard to confidentiality, safety, security and integrity of the assessment.

- **Fair** – the assessment is set at the right level and is inclusive for all learners. Differentiation can ensure any special needs are taken into account without putting the learner at an unfair advantage or disadvantage. It is best to check any changes you make with your organisation as you may need formal approval.

- **Reliable** – an assessment would be perfectly reliable if independent assessors, using the same criteria, marked and graded a piece of work exactly the same.

- **Sufficient** – an assessment where the full range of performance is identified in the standards covered. The evidence may need to show competence over a period of time and in a range of contexts.

- **Valid** – an assessment should assess the right skill and knowledge at the right level, for example, demonstration of a practical skill or conversation for a foreign language.

Assessments must be run according to external or internal guidelines, awarding organisation criteria and ideally in such a way as to motivate learners. Feedback to learners and colleagues should be constructive, whilst maintaining fair and measurable standards.

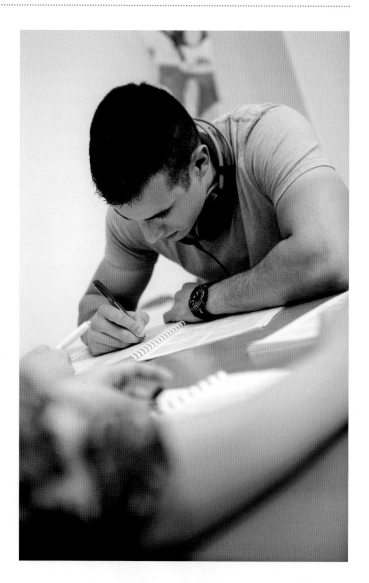

Use **SMART** to help you plan your assessments

 Specific – the assessment is designed to assess the criteria specified and no more.

 Measurable – the method of assessment is measurable against the assessment criteria.

 Achievable – learners can achieve the criteria at the right level.

 Realistic – the assessment method is valid, sensible, relevant and will give consistent results.

 Time-bound – appropriate time is allowed for the assessment process.

Ensure inclusivity and encourage diversity in your assessments by differentiating where appropriate, for example, a learner with a stronger reading/writing learning style can produce the evidence required by completing a written assignment, whereas another learner more strongly auditory in learning style may be able to provide the evidence with a recorded discussion with the assessor. Ensure the assessments are guided by the learning outcomes and that vocational assessments are relevant to the work setting.

Planning assessments

Unit 2: 3.2 Unit 3: 1.4 2.1

Check that your venue, resources and room layout are right for the assessment, for example, tables are set the correct distance apart for a formal exam. In addition, don't forget to follow your organisation's regulations and fulfil their requirements. You may be able to plan the assessment method, time and date with the learner, if it isn't completely prescribed by the organisation or awarding organisation. You may also want to agree time, date and other factors, for example venue, with the learner's employer or other teachers in your organisation.

It is important to communicate well with others who are involved in the assessment process, so that things run smoothly, efficiently and within the awarding organisations requirements. Others who may be involved could be the learners' organisation, administrators, exam invigilator, other learners involved in scenario/simulation type assessments, clients or patients involved in clinical assessments. It needs to be clear whose responsibility it is to inform all involved. Often it is the administrator and teacher but it may be useful for the learner to take some responsibility for their assessment. When differentiating to meet learners' needs, you will need to plan how best those adaptations will work in that venue with least disturbance to anyone else.

When required, assessments may need to give learners opportunities to demonstrate the depth of their knowledge or skill, especially for graded assessments.

Ways to differentiate in assessments to meet individual needs of learners:

- use different fonts and colours on typed material

- rearrange furniture

- use a more accessible venue

- provide resources or ICT facilities, for example a recording device

- language adaptations, for example sign language, braille or a translator

- ask questions verbally rather than give a written question paper

- allow extra time

Sources of information

Unit 3: 2.3

Learners and others involved in the assessment process need to be aware of where they can access information regarding the venue, timings, assessment method, assessor/s, grading process, appeals process etc. Information on costs, learner's progress etc may need to be available to whom it's relevant, for instance, the learner's manager, employer, training provider or assessor.

Activity:

How will you assess your learners in your micro teach session?
Add this to your lesson plan. Which three methods of assessment do you think you will use most when teaching your specialist subject?
Explain how you might adapt those assessment methods to meet individual learner's needs and fulfil the assessment criteria.

Main methods of assessment

Unit 3: 1.1, 1.2, 1.3, 1.4, 2.1

Key

AC = Assessment Criteria   **SLO** = Specific Learning Outcomes

Characteristics	Strengths	Limitations	Adaptations
Coaching – guides learners through problems or practical skills.	Embeds skills and understanding with good clear guidance. Use of touch/verbal and demonstrative skills.	Can be time consuming. Can leave the learner without the skills if not coached properly.	Differentiation needed but each learner must have equal chance to learn and get feedback.
Discussion – uses a range of written and spoken questioning techniques to find out if learners have the necessary knowledge.	Can be one to one or with the whole group allowing for full participation in discussion and questions.	Some learners may not participate, others may be too vocal. The discussion may get side tracked and not fulfil the AC.	The assessor must keep the group focussed and to time. It may be necessary to have smaller groups or mediate according to ability and needs.
Essays – a written discussion/text.	Allows learners to develop ideas, understanding and critical thinking skills. Can be used to measure literacy skills. Best for theoretical subjects or creative writing.	Literacy skills need to be fairly high. Learners with a SpLD may be at a disadvantage. Potential for plagiarism. Marking is time consuming and standardisation of grading may be an issue.	Needs a clearly designed formula for marking and grading. Let learners know the AC and show them good and bad examples of essays. Extra time for those with an SpLD.
Journals – learner keeps a diary or log to note progress and reflections during the course.	Helps to focus and think around the course. They learn to relate theory to practice. Helps to develop self-awareness and self-evaluation skills. More suited to higher-level courses/qualifications.	Tempting to be primarily subjective, or a simple log of events rather than objective and analytical, which is its purpose. Time-consuming to read.	It may be best to ask specific, guiding questions to aid and help develop each learner's reflective skill. Can be recorded as an audio file.
Learner statements – learner's account of work done towards the qualification units to date.	Can be used to support the evidence of ongoing work, development and improvement in performance and practice.	May not be kept up to date. Learner may not have sufficient opportunity in work setting to gather necessary experience to meet the AC.	May be recorded in various ways to suit the learner's needs e.g. electronic recording, written reflections or a log.
Multiple Choice Question Papers (MCQPs) – learner chooses correct answer, usually from one of four possibilities.	Can test many subjects. If cleverly written can emphasise the important aspects of the course for the learner to retain SLO in the long term. Easy to administer and mark. Cost effective and objective.	Can be very time consuming and difficult to write. Is harder to test attitudes and higher thinking skills. Learners must be literate in and comprehend set language.	Reading aids may be required by some learners. MCQPs can be prepared in different fonts, colours, type size and languages to suit the individual.

Characteristics	Strengths	Limitations	Adaptations
Observations and skills tests – watching learners perform in the workplace and demonstrate practical skills as they do their job. Often used to formally test technical skills as part of a qualification and assessed by an independent assessor.	Real life and work skills assessed. May fulfil many AC at once. Can give the learner confidence, realising they can perform under the pressure of the assessment.	The learner may not perform well under the pressure of the assessment. Differing standards of the skill may be an issue.	Clear guidance needed to standardise the level of skill required. Some learners may need industry acceptable adaptations to equipment or time given to complete the task/skill test.
Peer assessment – learners receive feedback from others in their group, or one to one. Usually informal assessment to support learner development. Feedback can be written and/or spoken and discussed.	Encourages involvement, interaction and reflection. Can nurture camaraderie and support within the group. The group can learn from each others performances and feedback.	Some learners may be over-positive in order to support their peer. Some may be quite negative and allow their feedback to be personal. The performance and feedback may not fulfil the AC.	Useful to set ground rules and clear guidelines as to the AC to comment on. The assessor must keep the group and feedback focussed, also correct any misinformation. It may be necessary to mediate according to ability/needs.
Projects, assignments and case studies – written case studies, assignments and projects that have been compiled by the learner throughout the course.	They provide evidence of the learner's knowledge and attitudes. The learner must have written feedback and it is best practice to discuss that feedback.	They may not provide evidence of competence. Giving feedback may be time consuming. Literacy skills may hold some learners back.	Literacy aids may be useful for some learners. Some case studies and assignments may be recorded electronically or by formal discussion.
Quizzes – usually informal and can be written or spoken. Learners give short answers to questions.	Tests knowledge, retention and application. Easy and quick to compose. Can encourage learners to read the course book and conduct further research. Can be fun. An informal and non-threatening way to allow learners to see the gaps in their knowledge and the areas they need to revise or revisit.	Informal. Can be difficult to score. Harder for those lacking literacy skills. Can be done minimally or thoroughly by the learner.	Can be in different fonts, colours, type size and languages to suit the individual.
Q&A session – learners answer questions from the assessor/tutor. Often used throughout lessons to recap, revise and clarify the important aspects of the course.	Quick and efficient. Encourages learner to express knowledge verbally, not just through a demonstration or on paper. Good for revision and focus not just for assessment. Allows space for logic and attitude.	Sometimes questions can be unclear or posed so that the learner is setup for a fall rather than a win. This is unfair and can set learners and the group back.	Questions must be clear and posed with skill, so the answer is clear if known. Allow the learner to express the answer non-verbally too, for example through a demonstration.

Characteristics	Strengths	Limitations	Adaptations
RPL – assesses the learner's existing relative qualifications and evidence to see if they meet the criteria units of a new qualification.	Saves repetition of learning and assessing.	It can be difficult to assess whether prior learning is truly valid, authentic and current to satisfy the new standards without very detailed assessment. Time consuming.	It may be easier for both the learner and assessor to complete the new units, taking into account their learning needs highlighted from previous experience.
Scenario/simulation – setting a scene. Real life simulation and testing the learner's ability to apply their learning.	Chance to try out skills in a real life situation. Great for learners who will be using their skills regularly. Can test their knowledge and skills for complex situations.	Can be costly. The set scenario can be too extreme for some. There is a big difference between a real event and stage fright/exam nerves. It may leave some learners with little confidence.	There must be clear guidelines with health and safety aspects researched well and adhered to for all learners and their needs. Some adaptations may be necessary for access and mobility.
Self assessment – The learners evaluate their own performance. Requires self-awareness, awareness of the AC level and honesty.	Encourages sense of responsibility for own learning and develops reflective practice. Helps the learner identify areas that need development and achievements.	Some learners can be very harsh on themselves and some overstate their achievement. Can be difficult for some learners to identify and voice/word stronger and weaker aspects of their performance.	Useful to give the learner clear guidelines and questions to reflect on, so they learn to develop their self-assessment skills. Can be recorded as written form, report, or audio file by the learner or if necessary the assessor.
Test papers – set question paper – more formal than a quiz but with similar properties.	Can test many SLOs. Can test lower and higher order thinking. Cost effective and can be easy to design. Easily marked with set AC.	Can be time consuming to mark if not designed well. Literacy and language skills needed.	Questions and tasks must be set clearly. Reading/writing aids may be required, or test papers prepared in different fonts, colours, type size and languages to suit the individual.
Work products – the end result or product of the learner's real work is reviewed with discussion, observation or formal discussion.	Real work skills learned and with good feedback/coaching can be developed to a high standard.	The work-based teaching and coaching may not be as thorough as needed and so the end product may fail to reach the standard required.	Standardisation must be maintained. Some learners may need industry approved adaptations to equipment and machinery.
Witness testimony – a witness testimony/statement from someone who knows the learner very well and verifies existing knowledge and practice, similar to a reference.	Gives evidence to support observation and other assessment methods. Can be a useful way to confirm evidence of RPL.	Possible bias or prejudice from the witness. They must be properly qualified to judge the learner in the AC.	Verify the credentials of the witness and authenticity of the testimony.

Principles of giving feedback

Unit 2: 4.3 Unit 3: 2.1, 3.1, 3.2, 3.3

Giving good quality, positive and constructive feedback is very helpful in establishing a good working relationship with learners. It is an essential tool that needs to be used well and a skill that teachers need to develop, as feedback given in the wrong way can be detrimental to the learning process. If carried out well, feedback can be motivational. Whatever form your feedback takes it should be:

Realistic – so that any goals set as a result of the feedback are achievable. You may need to adapt your assessment method to meet individual learner needs.

Negotiable – allowing the learner opportunities to explain their reaction. Involving the learner can enable them to take responsibility for their own learning thereby empowering and motivating them for their ongoing learning.

Specific – commenting constructively on specific aspects, not generalising. It is good practice to set a time limit on feedback sessions.

Feedback can be given in a variety of ways.

For instance:

Marking – feedback can be given with returned work marked with comments from the teacher. This usually works very well and the advantages are:

- There is a record of the assessment

- The learner and the marker can agree on the outcome and it can be recorded

It is worth mentioning plagiarism here. It is a very serious academic offence, often resulting in being disqualified. The awarding organisation that accredits the qualification and the organisation through which it is achieved often have a strict policy on plagiarism.

Plagiarism is the act of passing someone else's work or ideas off as your own, or using their work and ideas without their permission and without accrediting the work to them.

Oral feedback can be used to supplement marked work where the teacher discusses the work with the learner. This allows for discussion between the learner and the teacher on such things as the learner's grades and the best way forward.

Skilled questioning is a way to give instant feedback and assess how well the lesson is going, discovering what your learners know already and if your learners have truly grasped the information. This is an ongoing form of assessment that will involve your learners throughout. This will require tact as your peers and learners may be sensitive to feedback.

Tutorial – a one to one discussion can guarantee the information exchange is confidential. However the main points of the discussion still need to be recorded.

Activity:

Think about feedback you have had in the past, both negative and positive. How skilfully do you think it was given? Was it constructive and even if pointing out a negative, used positively? Choosing a negative experience, how would you do it differently to be constructive and motivate the learner?

Reflective activity:

How do you remember feeling when receiving or giving feedback on the occasions described in the above activity? How big or small an impact did they have on you? Did they affect your future decisions and choices in learning or teaching?

Assessment decisions and feedback

Pass or fail; competent or referral; grading

Deciding whether or not a learner's work meets the required standards needs clear set criteria and guidelines, experience, subject knowledge and sensible judgement on the part of the assessor. The assessment criteria will be prescribed by the professional organisation, awarding organisation or employer. There may be a variety of decisions to be made. Some subjects may still have clear pass or fail classifications, for example a driving test, but it is common nowadays for results to be classed as a pass (can be termed 'competent') or a 'referral'. Referral means that there is more work for the learner to do before a pass can be accredited. The learner may need to resit the whole course, provide more evidence or just resit the assessment. If there is doubt about the authenticity of a learner's work, the assessor would need to follow their organisation's or awarding organisation's policy on plagiarism (see page 95).

Reflective activity:

How might you involve the learner in deciding how best to assess them?
How can feedback contribute to the assessment process?

Simple steps to making assessment decisions – Valid, Authentic, Reliable, Current and Sufficient (**VARCS**).

Ask yourself these questions of the learner's evidence:

 Valid: Does the evidence meet the learning outcomes and assessment criteria of the agreed standards?

 Authentic: Is the evidence the learner's own work?

 Reliable: Has a marking system been used that would result in an independent assessor reaching the same decision?

 Current: Is the evidence in line with up to date industry standards and guidelines?

 Sufficient: Is there sufficient evidence to prove the learner's competence to the standard required?

Peer feedback

Unit 3: 2.1 2.2, 3.1, 3.2, 3.3

An excellent way to involve learners in the assessment process is through peer feedback. Peer feedback is a good way to learn from your colleagues and them from you. Observation of each other's work skills, knowledge or teaching sessions, with verbal and written feedback, is an ideal method of informal or formal formative assessment. When part of a teaching team, it is good practice to observe each other teaching regularly to share best practice. It may be a requirement of your awarding organisation for the IQA to observe all of the members of the teaching team to ensure standardisation within your organisation, both in teaching practice, specialist subject and assessment. The EQA may ask for proof of this process when auditing.

You will be required to give feedback to your peers on your Level 3 Award in Education and Training course. While the following table is provided for giving feedback to other teachers, it is also useful for other forms of feedback, including self-evaluation.

Positive attributes

Positive attributes to look for when giving feedback to other teachers:

What	Why
Good planning – logical order of lesson	A logical flow of information avoids confusion.
Referring to lesson plans	To ensure that logical order is maintained.
Passionate and **enthusiastic** about the subject	The topic may not be new and exciting to the teacher but it is for the learner and a fresh enthusiastic approach is infectious!
Knowledge of the specialist subject	Knowledge of the subject also needs to be Valid, Authentic, Reliable, Current and Sufficient – VARCS
Variety of **teaching** and **learning** methods	A variety of inclusive teaching methods to suit all learning styles makes the lesson stimulating and suitable for all learners.
For practical subjects: **E**xplanation/**D**emonstration/**I**mitation/**P**ractice **(EDIP)**	A logical way to teach a practical lesson and good for strongly kinaesthetic style learners.
Repetition, repetition, repetition! Repetition of important information and practice	Repetition suits all learning styles, especially auditory. Practice with encouraging and skilful coaching embeds accurate kinaesthetic memory and boosts confidence.
Good sense of humour	Makes the course enjoyable and memorable. Relaxes learners and helps group cohesion.
Uses **examples** and **stories** (relevant to the subject and objective)	Allows learners to put the theory into a different context. The information is then relevant to a real situation. Allows visual learners to visualise the theory and situation.

What	Why
Lighthouse technique	Maintaining eye contact with all learners, so they are all included and helps to assess their understanding.
Question and answer technique (Q&A) Encourages two way communication	Develops two way communication keeping the learners interested and involved in the lesson. Enables the teacher to check that learning has taken place.
Pitching questions at the right level "Pose, prompt, pounce"	Prompting leads the learner to the answer and encourages thought and involvement. Powerful for memory and confidence as leaners realise they knew it already.
Asks questions of the whole group and smaller sections of the group	Excellent for inclusion and assessing learners. Promotes group coherence and helps to limit outspoken learners answering all the questions by encouraging quieter learners.
Always **positive** with learners suggestions/answers and at the same time giving accurate feedback.	Encourages learners to participate in Q&A. Avoids undermining a learner. Skilful teachers can be positive yet let the learners know the correct answer.
Uses simple and appropriate **diagrams, PowerPoint presentations or film clips**. Discusses and explains them	Useful for all learning styles and those with weaker literacy skills. Well chosen film clips enable the information to become real and relevant.
Colour association for mnemonics and use of upper and lower case letters	Easier for all learners to read but especially those with any degree of dyslexia. Engages Long Term Memory (LTM).
Using rhymes, songs or mnemonics with repetition	Helps engage the LTM.
Using some drama and roleplay (acting during the lesson)	Engages the LTM and exercises the VARK learning styles. Helps put the theory into context and makes learning more memorable.
Having a kinaesthetic element to a theoretical subject	Exercises the kinaesthetic learning style. Helps put the theory into context and more memorable.
Expression and power of voice	Variation maintains interest. Use to emphasise the important topics.
End of lesson recap	Helps learners identify the most important parts of the lesson – emphasises the information they need to remember.
Professional and approachable	Essential for: • the smooth running of any course • learning to take place • credibility of the trainer and company • good business

Features of constructive feedback

Unit 3: 3.1

When giving verbal feedback ensure it is:

Clear, in easy to understand language and in chunks of information that are relevant to the task or assessment criteria and factual. Ideally feedback is given immediately whenever possible.

Owned, that is from you. You cannot speak for anyone else (unless you are formally representing an organisation in a professional capacity). You can share ideas here rather than giving advice. It is useful to use language like 'I thought …' 'I felt that…'

Positive and constructive, people often tend to dwell on the negative but it is more constructive to seek the positive and give constructive comment on aspects that did not work or could be improved upon. A useful technique to use is to 'sandwich' your feedback starting with positive comments, then constructive criticisms and always finishing with something upbeat and encouraging. This tends to be a balanced and more motivating way of passing on the same ideas. Think of yourself as a critical friend.

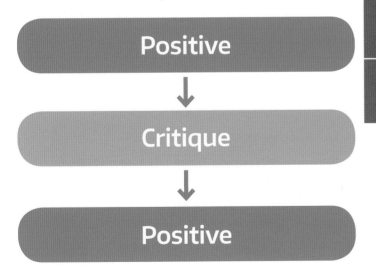

Positive

↓

Critique

↓

Positive

Activity:

Deliver your microteaching session.

Activity:

Give both verbal and written feedback to your peers on the course following their microteaching sessions using the criteria on *pages 97-98*. You are aiming to gather some skill in assessing others' teaching skills and giving feedback. This will in turn help you know what to look for in your own teaching and evaluate your own performance.

Activity:

Self-assess each completed assignment you do for your AET qualification. Be your own critical friend and check you have done everything asked of you and met the relevant criteria.

Self assessment and self-evaluation

Unit 2: 5.1, 5.2 Unit 3: 2.2

We all learn by self assessment, thinking something through and working out the best way of doing things. Think of something you are good at and in the process you have probably asked yourself:

- What am I trying to do exactly?

- What went well and why?

- What went less well and why?

- How could I do better next time?

Theorists such as Carl Rogers placed self assessment at the start of the learning process; what the learner learns, they learn for themselves. Kolb's learning from experience cycle also places heavy emphasis on self assessment.

What is very clear from all theories on learning and to some degree is perfectly obvious, is that when we learn, we remember something if we do it, think about it, process it and reflect on it further. It is important to get into the habit of self-evaluating and assessing your teaching sessions as it is a necessary part of your ongoing professionalism. Record keeping has a role here as you can reflect on and evaluate your development over time.

Reflective activity:

Why do you think it is useful to use both peer and self assessment?

Activity:

Self assess your microteaching session against standards for excellent teaching, use the Positive attributes table on page 96. Identify areas of improvement and areas of success.

Activity:

Self-assess each completed assignment you do for your AET qualification.

Be your own critical friend and check you have done everything asked of you and met the relevant criteria.

Record keeping, evaluation and assessment

Unit 3: 4.1, 4.2

We must keep accurate records of assessments:

- **Internally** (within your organisation) – for example to monitor each learner's progress from application and registration, through all types of assessment to completion and certification (where relevant). If all of their results are tracked it will help to identify areas of strength and weakness and also enables effective planning for ongoing learning. Tracking results may also highlight areas of the course that show a standard of success and excellence or have issues with quality and effectiveness that need to be reviewed. One of the main purposes of record keeping is that it helps in decision making by providing accurate evidence on various aspects of a course. For example, evaluation forms from learners and teachers as well as attendance records can help us to assess the course's effectiveness.

- **Externally** for example, your awarding organisation or funding agency will have an interest in your records for the purposes of auditing, standardisation and quality assurance. The awarding organisation will also have requirements as to which specific records need to be kept and for how long. In further education, quality assurance will play a large part in the retention of learners, their achievements and have a considerable impact on funding.

Standardisation and quality assurance

Standardisation is the process of ensuring consistency and fairness in teaching and assessing practice throughout your organisation. If more than one of you is teaching the same course, it is important to have standardisation meetings to develop and share good practice. It is wise to agree on the scheme of work, lesson plans, resources, assessment methods and procedures before the course runs. Thereafter, to help standardise assessment decisions and marking, the team can meet to compare and discuss their results. Double or blind marking, where you mark each others work to see if you conclude the same marks, is also a good way to ensure consistency.

Internal quality assurance

Also called internal verification, internal quality assurance must ensure the maintenance and improvement of assessments within your organisation. The IQA is a member of staff, qualified and experienced in the subject area and whose responsibility it is to validate the assessment decisions and practice of the team and deal with any problems that occur. They achieve this by checking random samples of each group's assessments. Internal moderation (remarking) is a form of internal quality assurance whereby if a problem is found within a sample group, learners' work may be reassessed and grades adjusted accordingly by the IQA. A learner may also refer their own work for moderation and each organisation should have procedures in place to enable such a request.

Completing your Level 3 Award in Education and Training and professional formation

> **"Share your knowledge. It is a way to achieve immortality"**
> *Dalai Lama XIV*

Towards the end of your course, complete a SWOT analysis (Strengths, Weaknesses, Opportunities and Threats) and action plan or summative profile to plan the next stages of your career and development.

Once you have gained your Level 3 Award in Education and Training you are on a very rewarding and professional career pathway. In terms of role progression, much of this will be dictated by your job role and is termed 'professional formation'. You can work towards a 'licence to practise' with the Education and Training Foundation (ETF), becoming a qualified teacher – Qualified Teacher, Learning and Skills – QTLS. QTLS status is on a par with QTS (Qualified Teacher Status) within schools. The Society for Education and Training (SET – the professional membership service of the ETF) states that it is 'committed to maintaining and improving the status and value of the QTLS process'.

In order to achieve QTLS you will need to gain the Level 5 Diploma in Education and Training. Once you have achieved the appropriate qualification you can work through your professional formation with the ETF to gain your professional status. The ETF can give you plenty of advice as to how you go about this when you are ready to do so. Remember to keep a log of your teaching hours and reflective practice as you progress throughout your career.

Continuing professional development

Unit 1: 1.2

"A teacher who loves learning earns the
right and the ability to help others learn."
Ruth Beechick, Easy Start in Arithmetic/K-3:

CPD is ongoing learning and development. CPD
is essential for professionals in keeping their skills
and knowledge up to date, so they are able to work
safely, effectively and legally. CPD may be gained by
formal or informal means and should be recorded and
documented as all professional bodies ask for evidence
as a condition of membership.

There will be changes now and then to your subject
specialism or teaching in general. All teachers need
to be up to date and knowledgeable in matters of
teaching, their subject specialism and policies pertinent
to their organisation and places of work. In 2004
the Government outlined its proposal to introduce a
'licence to practise' for all teachers and lecturers in the
Education and Training sector (Equipping Our Teachers
for the Future. DfES 2004). If you are working towards
a ATLS/QTLS you will need to provide evidence of your
CPD and reflective practice and continue to do so to
maintain your 'licence to practise'.

"CPD gives the public, learners, the teaching
community and the sector confidence that
teachers, trainers, tutors and assessors
are continuously improving their skills,
knowledge and expertise. CPD is the
hallmark of the professional".
(Institute for Learning, 2009)

CPD can be formal (for example a course or conference) or
informal (impromptu discussion with a colleague), planned
well ahead or opportunistic but the CPD that counts has to
show a real impact on your knowledge and practice. CPD
will enhance your job satisfaction too.

"Keeping us interested is keeping
us interesting"
(Orr 2011)

Activities that provide CPD are:

- reading trade publications in your area of work

- reading your organisation's news publications

- formal and informal meetings with colleagues

- meetings with internal and external quality assurers
  and moderating authorities

- e-learning

- teaching and subject specialist conferences

- observing/shadowing colleagues teaching

- evaluating feedback from learners and peers

- self-evaluation and reflective practice

Some useful organisations for general teaching matters that may improve your professional development are:

- Ofqual
- Education and Training Foundation
- The National Training Organisation – NTO
- Awarding Organisations – e.g. Edexcel, City & Guilds

Other useful sources of information for CPD are:

- The BBC
- The Teaching Channel on satellite TV
- Education supplements in quality newspapers

Some useful websites are:

- Success For All
- Department for Education
- Training Matters
- Training Foundation
- Ofsted
- Think, Educate, Share
- Ofqual

Reflective activity:

How does the thought of doing regular CPD make you feel? How does it feel to be part of a profession that continuously develops and adapts to meet the needs of individuals and society in general? Are you given opportunities for CPD at your place of work?

Activity:

Identify CPD activities you can carry out to improve your teaching practice.

Identify CPD activities you can carry out in relation to your subject specialism.

Identify CPD activities you can carry out in relation to your organisation and its policies.

References and further information

Read, H. 2011. *The Best Assessor's Guide*. Read On Publications Ltd. Bideford.

Rust. Chris- 27 June 2002 First published as *'Guide to assessment'*, in *Assessment strategies for Pop Music Performance*, 1999, University of Salford Dept of Music, F.

Appendix and References

Appendix – Award in Education and Training Units

The following are the LSIS theory units for the Level 3 Award in Education and Training. For ease of reference, each unit has been given a number. Please note that this number is solely for the purpose of this guide, to show the assessment criteria each section is fulfilling. When referring to these units in other books or websites please refer to the unit title and unit reference number.

Unit 1 – Understanding roles, responsibilities and relationships in education and training

Level 3 Credit Value – 3

Learning Outcome – The learner will:		Assessment Criterion – The learner can:	
1	Understand the teaching role and responsibilities in education and training.	1.1	Explain the teaching role and responsibilities in education and training.
		1.2	Summarise key aspects of legislation, regulatory requirements and codes of practice relating to own role and responsibilities.
		1.3	Explain ways to promote equality and value diversity.
		1.4	Explain why it is important to identify and meet individual learner needs.
2	Understand ways to maintain a safe and supportive learning environment.	2.1	Explain ways to maintain a safe and supportive learning environment.
		2.2	Explain why it is important to promote appropriate behaviour and respect for others.
3	Understand the relationships between teachers and other professionals in education and training.	3.1	Explain how the teaching role involves working with other professionals.
		3.2	Explain the boundaries between the teaching role and other professional roles.
		3.3	Describe points of referral to meet the individual needs of Learners.

Unit 2 – Understanding and using inclusive teaching and learning approaches in education and training

Level 3 Credit Value – 6

Learning Outcome – The learner will:			Assessment Criterion – The learner can:
1	Understand inclusive teaching and learning approaches in education and training.	1.1	Describe features of inclusive teaching and learning.
		1.2	Compare the strengths and limitations of teaching and learning approaches used in own area of specialism in relation to meeting individual learner needs.
		1.3	Explain why it is important to provide opportunities for learners to develop their English, mathematics, ICT and wider skills.
2	Understand ways to create an inclusive teaching and learning environment.	2.1	Explain why it is important to create an inclusive teaching and learning environment.
		2.2	Explain why it is important to select teaching and learning approaches, resources and assessment methods to meet individual learner needs.
		2.3	Explain ways to engage and motivate learners.
		2.4	Summarise ways to establish ground rules with learners.
3	Be able to plan inclusive teaching and learning.	3.1	Devise an inclusive teaching and learning plan.
		3.2	Justify own selection of teaching and learning approaches, resources and assessment methods in relation to meeting individual learner needs.
4	Be able to deliver inclusive teaching and learning.	4.1	Use teaching and learning approaches, resources and assessment methods to meet individual learner needs.
		4.2	Communicate with learners in ways that meet their individual needs.
		4.3	Provide constructive feedback to learners to meet their individual needs.
5	Be able to evaluate the delivery of inclusive teaching and learning.	5.1	Review the effectiveness of own delivery of inclusive teaching and learning.
		5.2	Identify areas for improvement in own delivery of inclusive teaching and learning.

Unit 3 – Understanding assessment in education and training

Level 3 Credit Value – 3

Learning Outcome – The learner will:		Assessment Criterion – The learner can:	
1	**Understand types and methods of assessment used in education and Training.**	1.1	Explain the purposes of types of assessment used in education and training.
		1.2	Describe characteristics of different methods of assessment in education and training.
		1.3	Compare the strengths and limitations of different assessment methods in relation to meeting individual learner needs.
		1.4	Explain how different assessment methods can be adapted to meet individual learner needs.
2	**Understand how to involve learners and others in the assessment process.**	2.1	Explain why it is important to involve learners and others in the assessment process.
		2.2	Explain the role and use of peer and self-assessment in the assessment process.
		2.3	Identify sources of information that should be made available to learners and others involved in the assessment process.
3	**Understand the role and use of constructive feedback in the assessment process.**	3.1	Describe key features of constructive feedback.
		3.2	Explain how constructive feedback contributes to the assessment process.
		3.3	Explain ways to give constructive feedback to learners.
4	**Understand requirements for keeping records of assessment in education and training.**	4.1	Explain the need to keep records of assessment of learning.
		4.2	Summarise the requirements for keeping records of assessment in an organisation.

References

Books

Anderson, J. R. (1999). Second Edition *Learning and memory: An integrated approach.* New York: John Wiley & Sons.

Anderson, L.W. and Krathwohl, D.R. (eds.) (2001) *A Taxonomy for Learning, Teaching and Assessing*: A Revision of Bloom's Taxonomy of Educational Objectives New York: Longram.

Armitage, Bryant, Dunnill, Hammersley, Hayes, Hudson, Lawes. (1999) *Teaching and Training in Post–Compulsory Education*, Buckingham: Open University Press.

Bloom, B.S. (1956) *Taxonomy of Educational Objectives: Handbook 1,* New York: Longman Buzan, T.

Crisfield J. (ed) (1996) *The Dyslexia Handbook.* BDA Reading UK.

Francis, M. & Gould, J (2014) *Achieving Your Award in Education and Training.* Sage publications Ltd.

Gardner, H 1993 *Multiple Intelligences – the Theory in Practice.* New York: Basic Books.

Gravells, Ann (2014) *Award in Education & Training* revised edition London: Sage publications ltd

Gravells, Ann (2012) *Preparing to Teach in the Lifelong Learning Sector*, 3rd Edition, Exeter: Learning Matters Ltd.

Gravells, Ann (2009) *Equality and Diversity in the Lifelong Learning Sector*, Exeter: Learning Matters Ltd.

Gravells, Ann (2009) *Principles and Practice of Assessment in the Lifelong Learning Sector*, Exeter: Learning Matters Ltd.

Kolb, D. (1984) *Experiential Learning: Experience as the Source of Learning and Development*, Upper Saddle River, NJ: Prentice Hall.

Laird, D (1985) *Approaches to Training and Development*, Harlow, Addison Wesley.

Lee, J (2002) *Making the Curriculum Work for Learners with Dyslexia*, The Basic Skills Agency.

Maslow, A (1987) *Motivation and Personality 3rd Edition,* Harlow: Pearson.

Miles Prof. T.R. (1993) *Dyslexia: The Pattern of Difficulties (Second Edition),* London: Whurr.

Peters Coffield, F., Moseley, D., Hall, E., Ecclestone, K. (2004). *Learning styles and pedagogy in post-16 learning. A systematic and critical review.* London: Learning and Skills Research Centre.

Peter, LJ and Hull, R (1969) *The Peter Principle: Why Things Always Go Wrong.* New York: William Morrow & Company, Inc.

Read, H. 2011. *The best assessor's guide.* Read On Publications Ltd. Bideford.

Reece I, Walker S (2007) *Teaching, Training and Learning*, 6th Edition, Houghton-le-Spring: Business Education Publishers Ltd.

Rogers CR, (1983) *Freedom to Learn for the 80s*, Columbos, OH:Merrill.

Skinner BF (1974) *About Behaviorism*, San Fransisco, CA: Knopf.

Tummons, J (2010) *Becoming a Professional Tutor in the Lifelong Learning Sector 2nd Edition.* Exeter. Learning Matters.

Journals

Maslow, A.H., *A theory of human motivation.* Psychological Review.

Dyslexia Checklist (Revised 1994). British Dyslexia Association. Reading UK.

Functional skills update 2, QCA, December 2005.

Newer Views of Learning – Types of Questions. Leslie Owen Wilson, 1997, updated 11/07.

Pashler, H.; McDaniel, M.; Rohrer, D.; Bjork, R. (2009). Learning styles: Concepts and evidence. *Psychological Science in the Public Interest* 9, 105–119.

Professor Chris Rust (2002). *Purposes And Principles Of Assessment.*

Robertson, B. *"Study Guide for Health, Social Care and Support Workers".*

Rudolf Berlin: *"Originator of the term dyslexia". Annals of Dyslexia* 23 (1): 57–63. doi:10.1007/BF02653841.

Rust. Chris- 27 June 2002 First published as 'Guide to assessment', in Assessment strategies for Pop Music Performance, 1999, University of Salford Dept of Music, F.

Tuckman, Bruce (1965). "Developmental sequence in small groups". *Psychological Bulletin* 63 (6): 384–99. doi:10.1037/ h0022100. PMID 14314073. Retrieved 2008-11-10. "Reprinted with permission in Group Facilitation, Spring 2001".

Vygotsky, L.S. (1978). *Mind and society: The development of higher psychological processes.* Cambridge, MA: Harvard University Press.

Websites

www.bdadyslexia.org.uk

www.dfes.gov.uk

www.dyspraxiafoundation.org.uk

www.et-foundation.co.uk

www.heacademy.ac.uk

www.irlenuk.com

www.ofsted.gov.uk

www.successforall.org.uk

www.tes.co.uk

www.anngravells.co.uk

www.acas.org.uk

www.hse.gov.uk

Glossary

AET – Level 3 Award in Education and Training.

Aim – a broad statement of what learners will achieve from the lesson or course.

Assessment – the process of measuring what has been achieved by learners and whether the course criteria have been met.

Assessment criteria – how the learner will demonstrate that the learning criteria have been met.

Awarding organisation – a national body that has the power to give you a qualification in order to recognise your learning.

ATLS – Associate Teacher in Learning and Skills.

CET – Level 4 Certificate in Education and Training.

Code of Practice – a set of written rules which explains how people working in a particular profession should behave set by their professional organisation.

Competence – being capable; the ability to perform a skill.

CPD – Continuing Professional Development is ongoing learning and development. CPD is essential for professionals in keeping their skills and knowledge up to date, so they are able to work safely, effectively and legally. CPD may be gained by formal or informal means and should be recorded and documented as all professional bodies ask for evidence as a condition of membership.

CTLLS – Certificate in Teaching in the Lifelong Learning Sector (now the CET).

Curriculum Vitae – the Latin name for a description of what you have achieved to date. Usually abbreviated to CV.

DET – Level 5 Diploma in Education and Training.

DfES – stands for the Department for Education and Skills, a government department.

Diagnostic assessment – a diagnostic assessment or skills test is designed to find out what level a learner is at in terms of a particular subject (often English, Mathematics or ICT, as a part of initial assessment), their abilities and if they have any learning needs.

Differentiation – using a range of different approaches and resources to meet the needs of all learners in the group, catering for their differences.

Diversity – people are different from one another i.e. their background, knowledge, age, gender, disability and any other characteristics.

Domain – an area or scope of knowledge or activity.

DTLLS – Diploma in Teaching in the Lifelong Learning Sector (now the DET).

Embed – to make something an integral part of something greater.

Equality – learners have an equal right to learn – the same rights and value as each other.

EQA – External Quality Assurer is an individual who represents an awarding body and checks the work of learners and teachers to maintain standards of quality.

ETF – Education and Training Foundation was formed to maintain high standards of professionalism and quality in teaching and training.

Evaluation – teachers and learners should be asked to give their appraisal, that is opinion on how effective the lesson or course was for them to determine its success and value.

Experiential – learning by doing or through experience.

FRQ – Framework of Regulated Qualifications – the framework for regulated qualifications in England, Wales and Northern Ireland.

Further Education (FE) – post-compulsory education. FE is usually undertaken to attain follow up qualifications necessary to attend university, or begin a specific career path.

Feedback – giving constructive information to a teacher or learner on their performance or coursework. It is an evaluative process.

Formative assessment – uses a range of formal and informal assessments to gauge a learner's progress during the course.

Functional skills – an umbrella title for core skills, mainly literacy, numeracy and ICT.

Ground rules – an agreed set of rules and code of conduct within a group.

Icebreakers – exercises to encourage learners to start to get to know each other, get involved and focused at the start of a lesson or group of lessons.

ICT – Information Communication Technology. The use of computers in a wide sense to aid and support learning.

IfL – Institute for Learning used to be the professional body for all teachers in the Learning and Skills Sector.

ILP – Individual Learning Plan – a learning plan specifically for an individual designed to set out how and when they will achieve their goals.

Inclusivity – being inclusive, including all components/people. In education being inclusive means that we involve all learners in relevant activities and do not exclude anyone, either directly or indirectly.

Induction – the process of introducing learners and anyone new to their new environment and its procedures.

Initial assessment – an introductory assessment of a learner to gauge their knowledge, level, suitability and any need for learning support.

Ipsative assessment – where the learner carries out ongoing comparisons and self-assessment of their own performance and development, with a set of standards on their own previous performance.

IQA – Internal Quality Assurer is an individual who checks the work of learners and teachers to maintain standards of quality within an organisation.

Learning Difficulties (LDs) – is more generalised than SpLDs and includes conditions that affect intelligence.

Learning Outcome – what the learner will know, understand and do as a result of their learning.

Learning styles – are the ways in which individuals naturally or through habit learn; how they best acquire and process information in learning situations.

Legislation – laws passed by legislative body, for example government, city council.

LSIS – The Learning and Skills Improvement Service (LSIS) was formed to accelerate quality improvement, increase participation and raise standards and achievement in the learning and skills sector in England. They were responsible for developing and providing resources that helped colleges and providers implement initiatives and improve quality. This was achieved by commissioning products and services, identifying and sharing good practice throughout the system, and providing tailored programmes of support.

MCQPs – Multiple Choice Question Papers, learner chooses correct answer, usually from one of four possibilities.

NVQ – National Vocational Qualifications, a range of work-based qualifications.

Objectives – are the stated detail of what is to be learned. They are written in a way that can be measured and specific, so that they can be assessed easily.

OFSTED – Office for Standards in Education (England). Inspectorate of schools and all childrens' educational services and social care.

Ofqual – Office of Qualifications and Examinations Regulation is a non-ministerial government department that regulates qualifications, exams and tests in England and vocational qualifications in Northern Ireland.

Points of Referral – other professionals and organisations to whom you may refer a learner to meet their individual learning needs e.g. Student Finance, Occupational Health Department.

PTLLS – Preparing to Teach in the Lifelong Learning Sector (now the AET).

Plagiarism is the act of passing someone else's work or ideas off as your own, or using their work and ideas without their permission and without accrediting the work to them.

QTLS – Qualified Teacher – Learning and Skills.

QTS – Qualified Teacher Status

Regulations – rules that govern procedure and behaviours and dictate how legislation should be carried out.

Resources – things that can be used to support or help a lesson.

RPJ – Reflective Practice Journal – a personal document in which the learner or professional reflects on their learning in order to engage in a process of continuous learning.

RPL – Recognition of Prior Learning – formally recognised learning and accreditation which will count towards a unit or award exempting the learning from re-doing the work.

RQF – Regulated Qualification Framework. The framework covers all the regulated qualifications, general and vocational in England, and vocational in Northern Ireland, and how they relate to each other. RQF replaces the Qualifications and Credit Framework (QCF)

SET – Society in Education and Training – the professional membership service of the ETF.

SpLD – Specific Learning Difficulties or some prefer 'differences', are a family of related conditions which together affect around 15% of people to some extent. They are neurological in origin and usually hereditary. SpLDs interfere with the way information is learned.

SSB, SSC – Standards Setting Body and Sector Skills Council are organisations responsible for developing national occupational standards and qualifications.

Standardisation – process of ensuring consistency and fairness in teaching and assessing practice throughout your organisation.

Summative assessment – is a final, often more formal assessment at the end of the course or lesson.

Unique Learner Numbers (ULNs) – a personal 10-digit number allocated to a Learner by the Learning Records Service (LRS). The ULN remains with the Learner throughout their life meaning all future credits and qualifications are linked together.

VARK – Fleming's learning styles: Visual, Auditory, Reading and Kinaesthetic.

Index